MW00795307

# Dilemmas in Social Work Field Education

# DILEMMAS IN SOCIAL WORK FIELD EDUCATION

## *Decision Cases*

Terry A. Wolfer
and
Melissa C. Reitmeier

COLUMBIA UNIVERSITY PRESS
NEW YORK

Columbia University Press
*Publishers Since 1893*
New York    Chichester, West Sussex
cup.columbia.edu



Library of Congress Cataloging-in-Publication Data
Names: Wolfer, Terry A., author. | Reitmeier, Melissa Catherine, author.
Title: Dilemmas in social work field education : decision cases /
Terry Wolfer and Melissa Reitmeier.
Description: New York City : Columbia University Press, 2021.
Identifiers: LCCN 2020050760 (print) | LCCN 2020050761 (ebook) |
ISBN 9780231201445 (hardback) | ISBN 9780231201452 (trade paperback) |
ISBN 9780231554107 (ebook)
Subjects: LCSH: Social work education. | Social service—Fieldwork. |
Fieldwork (Educational method)
Classification: LCC HV11 .W7145 2021 (print) | LCC HV11 (ebook) |
DDC 361.3071/1—dc23
LC record available at https://lccn.loc.gov/2020050760LC ebook record
available at https://lccn.loc.gov/2020050761

Cover design: Chang Jae Lee

These decision cases were prepared solely to provide material for class discussion and not to suggest either effective or ineffective handling of the situation depicted. While each case is based on field research regarding an actual situation, names and certain facts may have been disguised to protect confidentiality. The authors wish to thank the case reporters for cooperation in making their accounts available for the benefit of social work students and practitioners.

# CONTENTS

# TO INSTRUCTORS

As explained in the introduction to decision cases, the decision cases in this collection are open-ended and unresolved—and therefore different from the cases commonly used in social work education. Because they are explicitly designed to target field education, field directors and field coordinators can use them to train field educators (e.g., field instructors, task supervisors, field liaisons, faculty, and staff). No matter how much experience they have with the case method of teaching, most field directors and field coordinators who use these cases will benefit from the extensive teaching notes written for them. These notes are available at no cost but only to instructors (i.e., field directors and field coordinators) by emailing coursematerials@columbiauniversitypress.com.

The teaching notes will help instructors select particular cases to use and prepare to lead in-depth case discussions. To help with case selection, each note begins with a case synopsis, intended case use, and possible learning outcomes. To help with discussion preparation, each note provides possible discussion questions organized into four sequential categories: facts, analysis, action, and personal reflection. Each note also suggests possible activities to supplement the case discussions and recommends print, online, and media resources.

# ACKNOWLEDGMENTS

The original idea for this project emerged many years ago in conversation with Robert Jay Palmer while he was a doctoral student at the University of South Carolina (UofSC) and working in the Office of Field Education. But it took collaboration with Melissa C. Reitmeier, case method colleague and current director of field education, and funding by former Dean Anna Scheyett to bring it to fruition. Subsequently, many others contributed to creating this collection of decision cases. Besides the co-authors (listed elsewhere), we want to thank the students who assisted us by transcribing interviews, doing background research for the teaching notes, co-authoring teaching notes, reviewing cases for content and writing errors, and formatting cases and teaching notes for publication. They include current and former students at UofSC: Sara English, MSW, PhD; Brian Graves, MSW; Maria Hogan, MSW; Alexis Kandetzki, MSW student; Bailey King, MSW; Taylor Newman, MSW; Meredith C F. Powers, MSW, PhD; Tamara Estes Savage, MSW, PhD; Janessa Steele, MSW; and Betty Wilson, MSW, PhD student.

We are especially grateful to the social work field instructors who reported their experiences to us in lengthy, probing interviews. These interviews often focused on situations, relationships, and experiences that troubled them and required them to recollect and reflect on these experiences in considerable detail. Obviously, this case collection would not have been possible without their disclosures and would be less compelling without their honesty. To preserve their confidentiality, however, we cannot acknowledge them by name.

Thus far, we have used these cases in training sessions for field instructors at UofSC in the BSW and MSW programs, at Field Faculty Development Institutes at annual program meetings of the Council on Social Work Education, at regional workshops with directors of field education across the United States, at faculty development workshops on case method at several schools of social work, and at national case method teaching institutes. We have also used some of these cases in field seminars for BSW and MSW students and an MSW capstone course at UofSC. Each time we taught these cases, the case discussions with colleagues and students helped us refine and clarify the cases and teaching notes.

During the publication process, we appreciated the guidance and support of yet other professionals. At Columbia University Press, editor Stephen Wesley has been patient and persistent in guiding the manuscript through the editorial review process. Two anonymous reviewers provided thoughtful and detailed feedback that helped us improve the cases and teaching notes. Ben Kolstad and his team at KnowledgeWorks Global Limited provided copyedits that consistently smoothed and clarified the writing.

We are grateful to each of these people and for their contributions.

# INTRODUCTION TO DECISION CASES

For more than a century, social work educators have used cases to teach students (Fisher, 1978; Reitmeier, 2002; e.g., Reynolds, 1942; Towle, 1954; Wolfer, 2006). Over time, these cases assumed many forms, ranging from brief vignettes of only a few sentences or paragraphs to complex chapter-length scenarios.

Merseth (1996) identified three basic educational purposes for using cases: to provide examples or exemplars to *illustrate* practice, to serve as foci for *reflecting on* practice, and to offer opportunities to *practice decision-making*. With regard to the first, cases provide concrete and specific examples of how professional theories or interventions apply in practice situations, helping students understand both theoretical content and practice skills. During the past three decades, most social work casebooks provided cases for this purpose (e.g., Arguello, 2019; Haulotte & Kretzschmar, 2001; Holosko, 2018; LeCroy, 2014, 2015; Rivas & Hull, 2003; Silver, 2019; Suppes & Wells, 2017).

---

This introduction is a revised and updated version of "Introduction to the Cass" in *Dying, Death, and Bereavement in Social Work Practice* (Wolfer & Runnion, 2008).

Cases have also been used, although less frequently, to stimulate student learning and reflection. These cases often include commentary about ethical issues and questions calling for personal reflection or writing. This use of cases is most common in liberal arts education at the undergraduate level (e.g., Burnor & Raley, 2017; Newton, 2013) and in ethics training for professionals (e.g., Campbell et al., 2009; Corey et al., 2018; Pence, 2016; Reamer, 2018; Rothman, 2013).

In contrast to their use to illustrate practice or reflect on ethics, cases can be used as a site to practice collaborative decision-making. This requires the use of open-ended *decision* cases, a particular type of case specifically developed for this teaching approach. Decision cases present students with unresolved situations that incorporate the challenges, ambiguities, and dilemmas of social work practice and require active decision-making on the part of students (e.g., Andersen & Schiano, 2014; Barnes et al., 1994; Cossom, 1991; Ellet, 2007; Lynn, 1999). Decision cases portray in great detail actual situations practitioners have encountered, thus reflecting the messy and ill-structured nature of professional practice. Typically based on an account by one practitioner (i.e., the case protagonist), decision cases often include conflicting statements (by the various participants involved), time constraints, competing ethical values, extraneous details, and incomplete information (i.e., only the information that was available to the practitioner at the time).

Because decision cases are open-ended, they do not tell students what the practitioner ultimately did or how the case turned out. For that reason, decision cases compel students to use their analytic and critical thinking skills, exercise professional judgment, reinforce and expand their knowledge of social work theory and research, and test their common sense and practice wisdom as they conceptualize the case. Ultimately, they identify and analyze complex, deeply layered problems; evaluate several possible and feasible solutions; and formulate a research-informed intervention based on a well-reasoned and thoughtful analysis. Given the nature of social work practice, it is not surprising that over the past twenty years cases designed for practicing collaborative decision-making and making professional judgments have proliferated in social work education (e.g., Busch-Armendariz et al., 2017; Franklin et al., 2019; Scales et al., 2002; Scales & Wolfer, 2006; Wolfer et al., 2013; Wolfer & Huyser, 2010; Wolfer & Runnion,

2008; Wolfer & Scales, 2006). This casebook presents a set of such decision cases.

## WHAT DECISION CASES ARE NOT

Just to be clear, it may be helpful to point out what decision cases are not.

First, decision cases do not require a deficits-based or problem-focused approach to social work practice, often associated with diagnostic models or approaches that evolved from diagnosing patient pathology. Despite the fact that decision cases explicitly invite problem-solving—in the sense of solving a puzzle or responding to a challenge—they do not require or imply a problem-focused approach to practice—in the sense of having a primary focus on pathology or requiring use of a medical model. For that matter, decision cases also do not require or imply a solution-focused approach—if that refers to a currently popular brief treatment approach. Readers may actually assume a strengths perspective when discussing decision cases. Be aware, however, that either a problem-focused or a strengths perspective can be too dichotomous (McMillen et al., 2004), distorting the reality of a case situation and potentially causing readers to overlook important aspects of the case. Case discussions benefit from having multiple perspectives in play.

Second, decision cases purposefully do not illustrate particular theories or intervention approaches. They seldom include much explicit theory unless the protagonist mentions it when reporting the case. Instead, they are designed to provide detailed descriptive data (i.e., context) about actual situations for use in case method teaching. As a result, students and instructors are free to apply whatever theories they find useful. In fact, they will usually find it necessary to use different theories to make sense of a situation and to decide how to respond. For students, this will illuminate the connections between various theories and practices. Students and instructors can draw potential theories from several sources. For that reason, to prepare for particular case discussions, instructors may (1) refer students to previous course materials or past experience, (2) assign them new readings on theory or intervention approaches, or (3) require them to research appropriate resources on their own (much as they must do in the field following graduation). While case discussions seldom provide theory directly, they often clarify the fundamental importance of applying theory to practice—as students recognize the power of theory to provide them a "handle" on complex situations—and also offer a means for understanding and assessing the relative value of alternative theories and intervention approaches—as students propose and consider various alternatives.

Third, decision cases do not imply that social workers can or should solve a problem without remainder (i.e., unambiguously, completely, permanently, for all parties). On the contrary, the best decision cases are ones about which competent practitioners will disagree, much like they do in everyday practice. Obviously, decision cases stimulate efforts to resolve problems. When we refer to resolving a problem, however, that is not to imply that all problems can be solved but simply to acknowledge that social workers must decide how to proceed from the point at which they find themselves. Further, such decision-making will tend to be more effective if social workers take account of the underlying and interlocking reasons that have created or exacerbated the problem and address these in their decisions. Increased decision-making skill is a major learning outcome from the use of decision cases (Lundeberg et al., 1999; Milner & Wolfer, 2014; Wolfer, 2006).

Fourth, decision cases generally do not report how the case turned out. Pedagogically, the open-ended nature of the cases provides a powerful incentive for problem-solving. It also better replicates what students will experience in practice: they, too, will need to make difficult decisions with limited and ill-structured information, under time constraints, and with uncertain consequences. Usually, they will have to make decisions going forward rather than have the luxury of hindsight to critique decisions by other professionals. In that way, discussing decision cases emulates practice and helps prepare students for exercising professional judgment in professional practice.

Finally, decision cases do not necessarily portray best practice. Each case includes a disclaimer: "This decision case was prepared solely to provide material for class discussion and not to suggest either effective or ineffective handling of the situation depicted." Rather than illustrate effective practice, decision cases portray challenging, unresolved dilemmas for group discussion and collaborative problem-solving. Because they are based in practitioners' experiences, they also present situations from the perspectives of the people who reported them. As a result, the cases deliberately include stereotypes, professional jargon, and pejorative or outdated language, and they reflect explicit or implicit biases as reported by the protagonists. In this way, the cases accurately portray what students and practitioners encounter in professional practice. When included in the cases, this content provides opportunity for instructors and students alike to problematize such information in discussions and to practice resisting it, just as ethical, competent people must do in professional practice.

## GENERAL CASE METHOD LEARNING OUTCOMES

The cases in this collection are decision cases focused on field education. Properly used, they provide opportunities for the general types of learning associated with case method discussions. As suggested by Barnes, Christensen, and Hansen (1994), decision cases help learners* adopt at least six aspects of a professional practitioner's point of view: (1) a focus on understanding the specific context, (2) a sense for appropriate boundaries, (3) a sensitivity to interrelationships, (4) an ability to examine and understand any situation from a multidimensional point of view, (5) an acceptance of personal responsibility for the solution of organizational problems, and (6) an action orientation (pp. 50–51). Writing as business educators, they argue that case method instruction helps learners develop an applied, "administrative point of view" (p. 50). The concept of an administrative or practitioner point of view shifts attention from what learners know to how they can use their knowledge. We refer to this as "thinking like a social worker" and will elaborate on it here.

First, the cases provide ample detail about the background and context of the practice situations they depict. As learners wrestle with the practice dilemmas in these cases, they come to understand the critical significance of context for problem framing and intervention.

---

* Going forward, we refer to the participants who discuss these field education cases as *learners* to distinguish them from the social work students with whom they work in field placements.

The relevant context varies across cases. For example, in particular cases the context will include some combination of culture, law, policy, society, community, agency, and university. Many of the cases also include specific dates because timing—whether internal (relative to events within the case) or external (relative to events in the broader environment)—is another important aspect of context. But not all the details turn out to be significant. Just as in actual practice situations, learners must sort through the contextual information, selecting what is relevant and significant and disregarding what is not. Occasionally, addressing the case dilemma will require them to gather information not provided in the case because overlooking some aspect of context may have contributed to the field educator's dilemma. Discussing these cases provides opportunities to practice both deciding what is relevant or missing and incorporating selected information into problem formulations and subsequent interventions.

Second, appropriate handling of the contextual information requires clear delineation of boundaries, sorting out what is separate and what is related. As learners wrestle with the practice dilemmas in these cases, they come to appreciate the need to distinguish certain aspects of each situation. For example, many of the cases turn on proper distinctions among social workers, field educators, field students, and clients; between individual clients and their families; between supervisors and supervisees; between field instructors and task supervisors or preceptors; between professions; or between organizations (e.g., field agency and university). Sometimes these boundaries do not seem apparent to the protagonist. In fact, lack of clarity regarding boundaries, roles, or both often contributes to the reported dilemmas. Of special importance, some cases cannot be resolved without specifying the client system. In field education, for example, the intersecting roles and commitments of field instructors, task supervisors, field liaisons, agency supervisors, and field directors or coordinators sometimes confuse students and professionals alike, creating or contributing to their dilemmas. Likewise, field educators must consider whether addressing a particular student need falls within the scope of their supervisory or educational role, expertise, or priorities. As suggested above, discussing these cases provides opportunities for learners to practice identifying and taking account of such boundaries in concrete situations.

Third, learners must consider the webs of relationships present in these cases in addition to understanding their background or context and the boundaries between subsystems. The cases portray relationships on multiple levels. Quite concretely, for example, the cases depict relationships involving clients, colleagues, supervisors, professional work teams, and organizations. These human relationships reflect the subtleties of culture, behavior, cognition, emotion, and motivation. The cases include both spoken and internal dialogue to more fully and concretely portray how the field educators who reported the cases experienced these situations and relationships. More abstractly, the cases also depict relationships between programs and policies, between professionals and host organizations, between events and their temporal context, and between theory and practice. In general, learners must interpret the "raw" data provided in the cases to draw their own conclusions. Where the cases include assumptions held or conclusions drawn by the protagonist or other persons in the case, learners must decide what to accept. Assumptions and conclusions always shape how people understand situations. Sometimes these very assumptions and conclusions inadvertently contribute to the issues and root problems.

Relationships serve not only as background for the cases. Several cases also reflect the evolution over time of helping relationships (with individuals, families, or groups) and especially of professional relationships (in supervision, work teams, or education). Whatever has contributed to the current dilemma, the field educator must decide what to do next. Just as in real life, there is no opportunity to go back in time to revise these relationships; change is possible only from the current point forward.

Fourth, while all but one of the cases were based on interviews with individual field educators (who are also social workers), they do not provide information on the protagonist's perspective alone. As much as possible, the case-reporting interviews explored perspectives held by other participants, as reported by the field educator. For that reason, the cases include other perspectives as these were filtered through the eyes and ears of the protagonist. While most of the cases involve relatively new field educators, a few depict the experiences of a field student, supervisor, or administrator. As a result, the cases may be useful for experienced field educators as well as novices. Whatever the perspective, the cases often include detailed dialogue that reflects differences in perspective and that invites interpretation.

Fifth, the cases demonstrate the essential role of the field educator. Each case poses one or more dilemmas experienced by the field educator who reported the case, highlighting that educator's critical roles as decision-maker and actor in the case. Often the reporting field educator was the only person who could intervene in the particular situation. Choosing not to intervene was seldom a real option and would, of course, carry its own consequences. Furthermore, the field educators often labored under time pressure caused by some imminent event that required their decision and intervention. Because the cases are drawn from actual field education scenarios, the field educators not only must decide under time pressure but also must often do so with incomplete information. As much as possible, the cases attempt to provide full information about the context for decision-making (i.e., personal, professional, organizational, and policy factors) of which the field educators were aware at the time.

In addition, many of the cases implicate the field educators themselves in the decision-making context. In other words, these detailed cases often reflect how the field educators' personal background, education, professional training, previous work experience, and time at their current job may each contribute to their preparation and ability to respond. More specifically, the cases reflect how the field educators' personalities, values, ethics, knowledge, and skills influence their decision-making. Discussing these cases will help learners understand how their own personalities, values, ethics, knowledge, and skills limit, focus, or enhance their understanding of and decisions about particular cases. In short, reading and discussing these cases will help learners better understand how the self of the field educator affects professional practice.

Sixth, the cases clarify the necessity of moving from analysis to action. Whether or not the information appeared complete and clear, the field educators had to make decisions and act. In many cases, the situation could not wait. For example, a semester or academic year was ending or some other deadline was looming, and that left limited time for deciding and then intervening. As suggested earlier, not deciding or not intervening is also a kind of intervention, with its own set of consequences; the choice not to act should be the result of the same careful consideration given to more active intervention and should not be the default position. At the same time, the case discussions often explore the potentially harmful consequences of ill-considered or precipitous action. In that way, discussion of these cases can help learners understand the fundamental necessity of deciding and the importance of doing so based on a thorough analysis of available data.

## SPECIFIC FIELD EDUCATION LEARNING OUTCOMES

In addition to helping learners "think like a social worker"—a skill that is vital in any area of social work practice—the cases in this collection provide a vehicle for social work field educators and/or students in field placement to develop their understanding of the educator role in field education and the rich complexities involved. Although case method teaching in general is aimed at helping learners integrate and apply knowledge they already have, as in actual practice, it also requires learners to identify gaps in their knowledge and take necessary steps to fill those gaps, under similar time pressures.

As a whole, this collection of field education cases portrays the range of experiences social workers may confront as field educators, whether in the specific role of field instructor, task supervisor, field seminar instructor, field liaison, field director, or field coordinator. Some of these decision cases may also help social work students understand the complex and varied roles of those involved in their social work field education program. For these reasons, the decision cases presented here represent a range of common field settings such as schools, hospitals, nonprofit agencies, correctional institutions, and residential facilities. In addition, one case comes from an international setting, providing a unique perspective on cross-cultural issues and conflict with parallels in North America. The cases present multiple issues common to field education, where performance issues often intersect with communication and supervision issues. Additionally, role confusion is an expected issue, as is how supervision is used (or not) and/or implemented across multiple levels (e.g., field instructor to student; field liaison to field instructor, student, or both; employer to employee [field instructor]). In some of these cases, termination or corrective action is expected for students but is not the singular focus because decision cases allow us to glimpse parallel processes across systems. This minimizes the mistaken attribution of pathology to individual participants in the case (e.g., student, field instructor, and field program staff). In fact, these cases reveal the complex nature of field education and the roles its many moving parts play in soundly educating future social workers. Some of the cases reflect common challenges of field education, such as helping a student overcome self-doubt when starting out in field placement or providing supervision when a student is not receptive to corrective feedback. But other cases address students' serious personal challenges, ranging from their inability to achieve an educational outcome or meet a minimum competency to their problems with addiction, and how field educators remediate these issues.

In cases where corrective action or termination is expected, there is opportunity to dissect the role of those involved in the case and the protocols the social work program has established to mitigate negative fallout, to support the student educational process, and to maintain respectful relationships with community partners. This allows field programs the opportunity to teach across the policies and procedures of their respective field models (covering, e.g., transportation of clients in student vehicles, field attendance, the definition of direct practice hours, and protocols for problem resolution in the field practicum), as well as to dive into common experiences students, field instructors, task supervisors, and field liaisons may experience while engaging in an internship (e.g., addressing underperformance, seeking supervision, receiving constructive feedback, or resolving behavior problems). Cases present the decisions that field educators make related to the provision of supervision and what that should look like for the setting (whether on-site or off-site) and for different types of students, the fit and performance of students by setting type, the requirements imposed by specific types of organizations (e.g., lack of privacy) as they relate to the student's ability to meet learning contract goals and comply with the National Association of Social Workers (NASW) Code of Ethics, and the tensions inherent in decisions involving multiple leaders (e.g., field instructor, task preceptor, agency head, field office staff, and field director) and those involving multiple students with individual learning needs.

Field educators—including field instructors, task supervisors, others working at the organizations where social work students complete their practicums, field liaisons, field seminar instructors, field directors, and field coordinators—need a working knowledge of the field practicum model and the field program's course syllabi, policies, and procedures, as well as an idea of the complex issues that often arise when mentoring social work students in field education. Further, they need a clear understanding of the limitations of their knowledge and scope of practice. They must be familiar with the legal protections for not only client choices but also student choices (e.g., the Family Educational Rights and Privacy Act and the Americans with Disabilities Act) and the issues involved in terminating or providing corrective action to social work students depending on how risk and liability are determined and by whom. In addition, they must be equipped to resolve a wide range of dilemmas in the moment in light of ethical principles—specifically, the NASW Code of Ethics. They must have the educational, supervisory, and management knowledge and skills to mentor and lead social work students into the workforce. They also must understand the current day-to-day functioning of individuals, families, groups, organizations, communities, institutions, and society and be prepared to help students deal with the real pressures they will face when they graduate. Working their way through these cases provides field educators and field students an opportunity to acquire factual information, integrate it with their prior knowledge and experience, apply it to specific/actual situations where their knowledge is still likely to be incomplete, and reflect on their own values, beliefs, feelings, and life experiences as these affect and are affected by the situations portrayed in the cases.

Many of these field educator decision cases connect directly with the 2015 Educational Policy and Accreditation Standards of the Council on Social Work Education. More specifically, field educators who are trained using these decision cases will be better equipped to help students apply generalist (foundation, BSW) and advanced generalist (advanced, MSW) knowledge, values, and skills to demonstrate the social work competencies and practice behaviors required by their school's social work field education program.

Additionally, using cases to train field educators will help programs encourage field educators to consider their use of field supervision; their ability to effectively mentor and supervise students (and the difference between the two); their effective and appropriate professional use of self in all phases of practice activities, including supervising students; their own or their organization's delivery of culturally sensitive social work practice, including appreciation and respect for diversity of gender, race, nationality, religion, ethnicity, sexual orientation, and differential ability; their effective use of communication skills (written and oral) with a variety of client populations, colleagues, and community members; and their adherence to the field education policies, models, and practices of the school of social work.

## DIVERSITY WITHIN THE COLLECTION

This casebook is based on research funded by a Dean's Teaching Award for *Enhancing Social Work Field Education: Decision Cases for Field Educators*—awarded by Dean Anna Scheyett and the College of Social Work at the University of Social Carolina. For budgetary reasons, many of the cases come from the southeastern United States and reflect regional demographics. Nevertheless, we sought diversity on a variety of demographic dimensions (e.g., gender, age, race/ethnicity, field-setting type, populations served, presenting field issues, and status of field student). In addition, the cases incorporate a variety of ethical, technical, and medical issues related to field education. The case matrix following this introduction identifies selected dimensions of the decision cases and reflects their diversity and complexity.

While these decision cases include students from a relatively limited range of demographic and cultural groups, what field educators learn about specific diversities may be secondary to what they learn about how to take account of diversities in field education. In other words, though content knowledge is necessary, it is not sufficient for decision-making in these cases or in professional practice. Field educators can learn to take account of diversity by dealing with familiar as well as unfamiliar types of diversity. For example, enlightening thought experiments result from considering how a case might differ if some demographic element was altered (e.g., if a protagonist were male rather than female or if a student were African American rather than white).

## CONCLUSION

This collection of decision cases will provide stimulating and challenging opportunities for you to practice professional social work decision-making, especially as it relates to field education. The cases may provide new information about field education—in general or at other social work programs in particular—as well as other aspects of professional social work practice. In addition, they will help you appreciate how field education issues may crop up in many forms across diverse fields of practice, how they intertwine with other aspects of the situations, and how they often have profound implications for everyone involved. At times, the learning that results from discussing these cases may be somewhat uncomfortable and difficult, even distressing. However, this will better prepare you for becoming and growing as a field educator and especially will increase your sensitivity to and understanding of the complexities inherent in field education.

## REFERENCES

Andersen, E., & Schiano, B. (2014). *Teaching with cases: A practical guide.* Harvard Business Review Press.

Arguello, P. T. (Ed.). (2019). *Queer social work: Cases for LGBTQ+ affirmative practice.* Columbia University Press.

Barnes, L. B., Christensen, C. R., & Hansen, A. J. (1994). *Teaching and the case method* (3rd ed.). Harvard Business School Press.

Burnor, R., & Raley, Y. (2017). *Ethical choices: An introduction to moral philosophy with cases* (2nd ed.). Oxford University Press.

Busch-Armendariz, N. B., Nsonwu, M., & Heffron, L. C., with Rhodes, D. M., Wolfer, T. A., & Goatley, E. (2017). *Human trafficking: Applying research, theory, and case studies.* SAGE.

Campbell, L., Vasquez, M., Behnke, S., & Kinscherff, R. (2009). *APA Ethics Code commentary and case illustrations.* American Psychological Association.

Corey, G., Corey, M. S., & Corey, C. (2018). *Issues and ethics in the helping professions* (10th ed.). Cengage Learning.

Cossom, J. (1991). Teaching from cases: Education for critical thinking. *Journal of Teaching in Social Work, 5*(1), 139–155.

Ellet, W. (2007). *The case study handbook: How to read, discuss, and write persuasively about cases.* Harvard Business School Press.

Fisher, C. F. (1978). Being there vicariously by case studies. In M. Ohmer and Associates (Ed.), *On college teaching: A guide to contemporary practices* (pp. 258–285). Jossey-Bass.

Franklin, L. D., Kratz, J. R., & Gray, K. A. (2019). *Next steps: Decision cases for social work practice.* Routledge.

Haulotte, S. M., & Kretzschmar, J. A. (Eds.). (2001). *Case scenarios for teaching and learning social work practice.* Council on Social Work Education.

Holosko, M. (Ed.). (2018). *Social work case management: Case studies from the frontlines.* SAGE.

LeCroy, C. W. (Ed.). (2014). *Case studies in social work practice* (3rd ed.). Wiley.

LeCroy, C. W., & Anthony, E. K. (Eds.). (2015). *Case studies in child, adolescent, and family treatment* (2nd ed.). Wiley.

Lundeberg, M. A., Levin, B. B., & Harrington, H. L. (1999). *Who learns what from cases and how? The research base for teaching and learning with cases.* Lawrence Erlbaum Associates.

Lynn, L. E., Jr. (1999). *Teaching and learning with cases: A guidebook.* Chatham House.

McClelland, R. W., Austin, C. D., & Este, D. (1998). *Macro case studies in social work.* Families International.

McMillen, J. C., Morris, L., & Sherraden, M. (2004). Ending social work's grudge match: Problems versus strengths. *Families in Society: The Journal of Contemporary Social Services, 85*(3), 317–325.

Merseth, K. K. (1996). Cases and case methods in teacher education. In J. Sikula, T. J. Buttery, & E. Guyton (Eds.), *Handbook of research on teacher education* (2nd ed., pp. 722–744). Simon & Schuster Macmillan.

Milner, M., & Wolfer, T. (2014). The use of decision cases to foster critical thinking in social work students. *Journal of Teaching in Social Work, 34*(3), 269–284.

Newton, L. (2013). *Ethical decision making: Introduction to cases and concepts in ethics.* Springer.

Pence, G. (2016). *Medical ethics: Accounts of ground-breaking cases* (8th ed.). McGraw-Hill Higher Education.

Reamer, F. G. (2018). *The social work ethics casebook: Cases and commentary* (2nd ed.). NASW Press.

Reitmeier, M. (2002). *Use of cases in social work education.* Unpublished manuscript, University of South Carolina, Columbia.

Reynolds, B. C. (1942). *Learning and teaching in the practice of social work*. Farrar & Rinehart.

Rivas, R. F., & Hull, G. H. (2003). *Case studies in generalist practice* (3rd ed.). Cengage Learning.

Rothman, J. C. (2013). *From the front lines: Student cases in social work ethics* (4th ed.). Pearson.

Scales, T. L., & Wolfer, T. A. (2006). *Decision cases for generalist social work practice: Thinking like a social worker*. Brooks/Cole.

Scales, T. L., Wolfer, T. A., Sherwood, D. A., Garland, D. R., Hugen, B., & Pittman, S. (Eds.). (2002). *Spirituality and religion in social work: A source book of decision cases*. Council on Social Work Education.

Silver, M. S. (2019). *Forensic social work case studies: Personal injury, family, immigration, and criminal mitigation*. Lulu.com.

Suppes, M. A., & Wells, C. C. (2017). *The social work experience: A case-based introduction to social work and social welfare* (7th ed.). Pearson.

Towle, C. (1954). *The learner in education for the professions: As seen in education for social work*. University of Chicago Press.

Wolfer, T. A. (2006). An introduction to decision cases and case method learning. In T. A. Wolfer & T. L. Scales (Eds.), *Decision cases for advanced social work practice: Thinking like a social worker* (pp. 3–16). Brooks/Cole.

Wolfer, T. A., Franklin, L. D., & Gray, K. A. (2013). *Decision cases for advanced social work practice: Confronting complexity*. Columbia University Press.

Wolfer, T. A., & Huyser, M. (2010). *Grappling with faith: Decision cases for Christians in social work*. North American Association of Christians in Social Work.

Wolfer, T. A., & Runnion, V. M. (2008). *Dying, death, and bereavement in social work practice: Decision cases for advanced practice*. Columbia University Press.

Wolfer, T. A., & Scales, T. L. (Eds.). (2006). *Decision cases for advanced social work practice: Thinking like a social worker*. Brooks/Cole.

| | Using Relationships (A) | Triggers . . . Triggers . . . | Slippery Boundaries | Workplace Bully (A) | Is He Okay? | Reluctant Social Worker | Handling Adversity |
|---|---|---|---|---|---|---|---|
| **Population Served** | | | | | | | |
| Children and families | | X | | X | X | X | X |
| Adults | | | | X | | | |
| Older adults | | | | | | | |
| Across Lifespan | X | | X | | | | |
| **Field Setting Type** | | | | | | | |
| School | | | | | X | | X |
| Residential Treatment | | X | | | | X | |
| Hospital | | | X | | | | |
| Correctional | | | | | | | |
| University | | | | | | | |
| Non-Profit | X | | | X | | | |
| **Field Setting Services** | | | | | | | |
| Neighborhood/Community Advocacy | X | | | | X | X | X |
| Therapeutic Residential Services | | X | | X | | | |
| Discharge Planning and Coordination Services | | | X | | | | |
| **Protagonist Role** | | | | | | | |
| Field Instructor | X | X | X | X | X | X | |
| Field Liaison | | | | | | | X |
| Field Student | | | | | | | |
| **Protagonist Demographics** | | | | | | | |
| Novice Professional | | X | X | X | | | |
| Experienced Professional | X | | | | X | X | X |
| Novice Instructor | | X | X | X | | X | |
| Experienced Instructor | X | | | | X | | X |
| Male | | X | | | | | |
| Female | X | | X | X | X | X | X |
| White | | X | X | | | X | X |
| Black | X | | | | X | | |
| Asian | | | | | | | |

| | Who to Fire? | Conflicted Learners | No Way to Drive | He Won't Go There | Protecting Children | Brews and Field Instructor Blues (A) | Collateral Damage (A) | Whose baby? |
|---|---|---|---|---|---|---|---|---|
| **Population Served** | | | | | | | | |
| Children and families | X | X | | X | X | | | X |
| Adults | | X | X | | | | X | X |
| Older adults | | | X | | | | | |
| Across Lifespan | | | | | | X | | |
| **Field Setting Type** | | | | | | | | |
| School | | | | X | | | | |
| Residential Treatment | | | | | X | | | |
| Hospital | | | | | | | | X |
| Correctional | X | X | | | | | | |
| University | | | | | | | X | |
| Non-Profit | | | X | | | X | | |
| **Field Setting Services** | | | | | | | | |
| Neighborhood/Community Advocacy | X | | | | | X | X | |
| Therapeutic Residential Services | | | X | X | X | | | |
| Discharge Planning and Coordination Services | | X | | | | | X | X |
| **Protagonist Role** | | | | | | | | |
| Field Instructor | | X | X | X | | X | | X |
| Field Liaison | X | | | | X | | | |
| Field Student | | | | | | | X | |
| **Protagonist Demographics** | | | | | | | | |
| Novice Professional | X | | X | | X | X | X | |
| Experienced Professional | | X | | X | | | | X |
| Novice Instructor | X | | X | X | X | X | X | X |
| Experienced Instructor | | X | | | | | | |
| Male | | | X | | | X | | |
| Female | X | X | | X | X | | X | X |
| White | | X | X | X | | X | X | X |
| Black | | | | | | | | |
| Asian | | | | | X | | | |

| | Using Relationships (A) | Triggers . . . Triggers . . . | Slippery Boundaries | Workplace Bully (A) | Is He Okay? | Reluctant Social Worker | Handling Adversity |
|---|---|---|---|---|---|---|---|
| **Student Demographics** | | | | | | | |
| BSW | | | | X | | | |
| MSW | X | X | X | | X | X | X |
| Traditional student | X | X | | X | X | X | X |
| Older student | | | X | | | | |
| Male | | X | | | X | | |
| Female | X | | X | X | | X | X |
| White | | | | | | X | |
| Black | X | | X | | X | | |
| Latino | | X | | | | | |
| Asian | | | | X | | | |
| **Field Issues** | | | | | | | |
| Impairment | | X | | | X | | |
| Trauma | | X | | X | | | |
| Communication | | X | X | X | | | X |
| Power Struggle | X | | | X | | | |
| Performance | X | | X | | X | X | X |
| Conflict | | | X | | | | |
| Fit | | | | | | | X |
| Ethical/Cultural | | | | X | | | |
| Learning Contract | | | | | | | X |
| Accountability | X | | X | X | | X | |
| Student Learning | | X | | | X | X | X |
| Student Initiative | X | X | | | | X | |
| Supervision | | | X | X | | | X |
| Field Instructor Preparation | | | | | | X | |
| Behavior Contracting | X | | | | | X | |
| Social Media Use | | | | | | X | |
| Insurance Coverage | | | | | | | |
| Role Confusion | | | | X | | | |
| Legal | | | | X | | | |

| | Who to Fire? | Conflicted Learners | No Way to Drive | He Won't Go There | Protecting Children | Brews and Field Instructor Blues (A) | Collateral Damage (A) | Whose baby? |
|---|---|---|---|---|---|---|---|---|
| **Student Demographics** | | | | | | | | |
| BSW | | X | X | | | | X | |
| MSW | X | | | X | X | X | | X |
| Traditional student | X | X | X | | X | X | X | |
| Older student | | | | X | | | | X |
| Male | | | | X | | X | | |
| Female | X | X | X | | | | X | X |
| White | | | X | | | X | X | |
| Black | | X | | X | | | | X |
| Latino | | X | X | | | | | |
| Asian | X | | | X | X | X | | |
| **Field Issues** | | | | | | | | |
| Impairment | | | X | | | X | | |
| Trauma | | | X | | | | X | |
| Communication | X | X | | X | X | X | X | |
| Power Struggle | | X | | X | | | X | X |
| Performance | X | | X | | | X | | |
| Conflict | | | | | X | | X | |
| Fit | X | | | | | | | |
| Ethical/Cultural | | | | | X | X | X | |
| Learning Contract | | | | X | | | | |
| Accountability | X | X | X | | X | X | | |
| Student Learning | | X | X | | X | | X | |
| Student Initiative | X | | X | X | | X | | X |
| Supervision | | X | | X | X | X | | |
| Field Instructor Preparation | | | | | X | | | |
| Behavior Contracting | | | | | | X | | |
| Social Media Use | X | | | | | | | |
| Insurance Coverage | | | X | | | | | |
| Role Confusion | | X | | X | X | | | X |
| Legal | | | | | | | X | |

Dilemmas in Social Work Field Education

# 1

## USING RELATIONSHIPS (A)

*Tamara Estes Savage, Terry A. Wolfer, and Melissa C. Reitmeier*

Field instructor Precious Clarke sat at her desk with her head in her hands. It was late November 2009, and she was trying to piece together what had happened over the course of the semester. She loved her job at Action, Inc., where she was involved in community organizing and coalition building, and she usually loved being a field instructor. But this semester was different. In a few minutes, John Swann, the field liaison from the University of Georgia (UGA), would arrive to meet with Precious and Kadasha Hunter, one of her student interns, for the final time that semester. *I don't even know*, Precious worried, *if Kadasha will show up for this meeting.*

---

This decision case was prepared solely to provide material for class discussion and not to suggest either effective or ineffective handling of the situation depicted. While based on field research regarding an actual situation, names and certain facts may have been disguised to protect confidentiality. The authors wish to thank the case reporter for cooperation in making this account available for the benefit of social work students and practitioners.

Despite several confrontations, Kadasha was still not consistently showing up for her internship. She was missing deadlines, and she submitted work that was riddled with mistakes, which required Precious to make extensive edits. *I care about her*, Precious reminded herself, *and I don't want to keep her from graduating. I understand why she's struggling. What am I gonna say? I can't sell her out. I don't want to make it any more difficult for her. I'm afraid if she doesn't do well with me, they're gonna put her somewhere else. She's been through so much.*

## ACTION, INC.

Action, Inc., a community association in northeast Athens, Georgia, focused on fostering and strengthening the neighborhood, school, and community relationships in the school district and on crafting policy related to community problems. In 1996, the association played a major role in addressing gang activity in the district when it facilitated community meetings that led to collective action and ultimately resulted in a decrease in gang activity. The organization also worked to prevent substance abuse among youth and build on positive assets through youth leadership training. It had evolved over time to include a board of directors, an executive director, and twenty-five active volunteers.

## PRECIOUS CLARKE, DIRECTOR

Precious Clarke, an African American, graduated from UGA in 1996 with an undergraduate degree in interdisciplinary studies. While completing her degree, she worked full-time, from four P.M. to midnight, at True Comfort Care, a private, nonprofit residential center for people with developmental disabilities. After graduating, she was offered the position of service coordinator for clients with disabilities at the Gwinnett/Rockdale/Newton Community Service Board (GRN) in Wilkes County, some forty miles from her home in Athens. It was a demanding job because there were few services in Wilkes County for her clients, and she had a daily two-hour commute. Knowing Precious had a passion for social work, a colleague encouraged her to apply to the MSW program at UGA.

After she was admitted to the program, Precious resigned from GRN and began the search for another job to support herself. Because she was a part-time student with evening classes, she needed a position with daytime hours. Her search resulted in two job offers, and she chose a position as a maternal outreach worker at the Athens Housing Authority (AHA). She was still trying to understand her work responsibilities when her supervisor announced that Precious needed to attend community meetings at night. Because that conflicted with her night classes, Precious promptly resigned from AHA and took a position at Women's Services of Athens. As the coordinator of the Athens Awareness Team, she directed the interactive theater troupe and provided abortion counseling.

During these transitions, Precious dealt with significant stressors in her life. A roommate left without notice and without paying her share of two months' rent. More significantly, while Precious was in graduate school, three of her relatives died, two of her high school friends died in unrelated accidents, and a coworker committed suicide. As Precious reflected, "It seemed as if I was always either picking up the pieces of a mess or attending a funeral. It was like life was conspiring against my graduate schooling."

Precious continued to work at Women's Services of Athens, and during the second year of the part-time MSW program, the organization also became the site of her first internship. Things were going well until June, when the chief financial officer (CFO) of the organization was arrested for grant fraud. As a result, Precious's entire grant-funded department was dissolved in August. She was without a job once again, but now she was also without an internship. Faye James, the director of community services at Child and Family Services of Georgia (CFSG), had worked successfully with Precious on community projects and called to offer her both employment and an internship. Subsequently, when Faye left CFSG in February to take another job, Precious was promoted to director of community services. Precious completed an internship separate from her employment, and after she earned an MSW in 2000, she continued working at CFSG.

After working with CFSG for seven years, Precious decided to try something completely different, and in 2007, she moved to Atlanta and worked as an investment representative for Street Capital for six months—until the economy faltered in 2008. She quit and moved back to Athens, where she was hired by the CFO of the Family Service Center as the director for the Workforce Development Center. However, her tenure at the center ended abruptly when the CFO was arrested for financial mismanagement and, once again, her department was dissolved.

Then Precious turned to fellow sorority members for help finding work. In 2008, she became the director of Action, Inc., an agency whose purpose was to resolve problems facing youth in the Athens school system. There she worked with community members to find solutions before these problems manifested in schools, and she worked with the school system to address these problems through policy development.

## INSTRUCTING SOCIAL WORK STUDENTS

While holding these professional positions, Precious also sought opportunities to provide field education. In 2002, two years after receiving her MSW, she began supervising social work interns. By 2008, she had supervised sixteen social work interns from several colleges and universities in Georgia, as well as AmeriCorps and Vista volunteers. One year she supervised six interns at the same time. She enjoyed supervising students and developed a positive reputation with field directors. Precious reflected, "I have a history of taking students who needed extra attention." With colleagues, Precious described herself as "demanding, a little cold, task-oriented, but willing to work with students." She considered herself "very flexible with field" because she was in the community a lot. She also regarded herself as "having intense moments" because the job is fast-paced. To students she said, "If you talk to me, I will be your personal cheerleader. If you have any questions, you can talk to me about it. You can use field time to complete school assignments if you talk to me about it first."

In 2005, Precious began teaching as an adjunct instructor at UGA. She usually taught two or three classes per semester—sometimes more. Because her focus in graduate school was communities and organizations social work, she taught classes such as Theory and Practice in Organizations, Community Assessment and Empowerment Practices, and Evaluation of Community and Institutional Practices. She was flexible as an adjunct, too. She taught both undergraduate and graduate social work students. Because she could always be counted on when there was a last-minute need for a teacher, she was the go-to adjunct whenever the School of Social Work was caught in a bind. Precious also loved teaching and loved the students, and she regarded teaching as one of the best experiences in her life. She believed that it was her responsibility to ensure that students leave her class more knowledgeable and skilled than when they entered. She also believed students brought unique experiences that enriched the classroom. She had high expectations of her students in the classroom, just as she did in field. She did not accept end-of-semester pleas for more time on an assignment if a student suddenly popped up with an unlikely story, yet if a student spoke to her about personal difficulties throughout the semester, she was willing to help in any way possible. As Precious explained, "I hold their feet to the fire, but I'm still in contact with most of my students after the semester ends."

## TIMIKA DORSEY, GRADUATE STUDENT INTERN

In summer 2008, Precious, now the director of Action, Inc., told the Field Education Office at UGA, "I need a flexible student who can work independently because I will not be there all the time." The office recommended Timika Dorsey, an African American MSW student who had completed her undergraduate degree in psychology. After their initial interview, it was obvious to Precious that Timika was the right choice for Action, Inc. She was an excellent student in the classroom and, as Precious expected, in the internship. "Timika is perfect," Precious told colleagues, "the perfect field student." Timika learned quickly, worked hard, and consistently completed her assigned work correctly the first time, whether for her classes or for her internship. She was confident and readily asked for clarification when she did not understand a task.

## A CALL FROM THE FIELD EDUCATION OFFICE

In mid-October 2008, Precious was working at her desk when her phone rang. It was David Harris, director of field education at UGA.

"I need a favor," he began.

"Okay," Precious replied, with only a little hesitation in her voice.

"I'm calling you," David explained, "because a student, Kadasha Hunter, is having some trouble at the internship she's at now. She's an advanced-standing student in Communities and Organizations. I noticed that you had her in class last semester, so you already know her. I don't know if it's her or if it's the placement, but I want to give her an opportunity to kinda work some of this stuff out. The internship does not want her anymore." David paused. "Precious, you've taken students who have needed extra attention over the years."

Precious remembered Kadasha, who had been a student in her foundation macro community practice course during the summer semester. She was a weak advanced-standing student, but Precious thought she had worked hard.

"Yes," Precious replied, with only a bit of hesitation, "I'll give it a try."

After the conversation, Precious rummaged through her desk and found her grade book. She saw that Kadasha had gotten a C on the first major writing assignment. That reminded her of a striking admission Kadasha had made on the assignment. She had written: "I feel that my bachelor's program did not prepare me effectively to succeed in this master's program or even in the world. I know that my writing is weak, and it needs help. I seem to have excelled in this program, but I am struggling now with this assignment." *She was right*, Precious mused. *She assessed herself properly, and I felt bad about giving her the C. When she got her assignment back, she seemed really invested in wanting to do better. So I took a little bit of extra time with her that semester*, Precious recalled. *I would catch her after class to ask questions and offer writing tips: "Have you been to the writing center? Get a friend to look over your stuff. Read some fiction while you're on break; read something you like. Trust me—it'll make you a better writer. You'll get a better idea of how sentences are put together."*

"I feel like the two of us built a really good rapport," Precious said out loud. "I feel like I can help her now."

## STUDENT ARRIVING

The following Monday Kadasha arrived at Action, Inc. She was a twenty-two-year-old African American from a small Georgia town, and Precious remembered her as being tall with long, dark hair and a broad smile. However, when Precious saw Kadasha that day, she appeared weary and worn. *She's just like a little wounded animal. I have to embrace her and help her get through field. I feel bad for her.*

After Kadasha settled into the center, Precious and Kadasha had their first supervision meeting.

"Kadasha," Precious began, "you know after having been in my class that I have high expectations. I am going to push you."

"Precious, I am just so glad you're taking me," Kadasha replied.

"The schedule is flexible here, but I need you to keep track of your hours on the office calendar," Precious explained, "and keep me apprised of any changes in your schedule."

"Alright, I understand," Kadasha replied.

"I will work with you on your makeup hours," Precious encouraged. "We will get you what you need; you just gotta be ready for the work."

"Alright, thank you, Precious."

## THE FIRST FIELD LIAISON VISIT

Field liaison John Swann visited Action, Inc., during the first week of Kadasha's internship. He was a white social worker who had retired after working for most of his career at the Veterans Health Administration and who now had a contract with the UGA Field Education Office to serve as a field liaison. John, Precious, and Kadasha mapped out a plan for the remaining semester. They discussed how Kadasha would make up the field hours missed during the transition, and John offered his help as needed during the semester.

"I'll keep an eye on things," John promised. "I'll try to help things run smoothly."

## GETTING UNDERWAY

At the beginning, Kadasha showed up for the internship and turned in her work, and Precious provided any extra help that she needed. Precious purposely gave Kadasha the less difficult tasks and gave Timika the more difficult ones. Nevertheless, Precious still had to spend time revising any written work that Kadasha completed. During the first two weeks, Kadasha told Precious that she was having personal troubles. She was still struggling with the breakup of a serious relationship over the previous summer, and, in addition, she was having difficulties with her job at the AHA. As a result, Precious gave Kadasha a lot of flexibility with her hours and extended deadlines for her work as much as possible.

As weeks passed, however, Kadasha's performance deteriorated. She began to miss deadlines and not show up for the internship. Precious kept prodding, reminding Kadasha that she needed to complete her work. Eventually, Kadasha stopped giving Precious any work at all. During Kadasha's sixth week at the internship, Precious confronted her after she failed to submit an article for the organization newsletter that went out to all the schools and parents in the school district.

"Kadasha, what's going on?" Precious asked.

"I've been really stressed out," Kadasha explained. "They changed my work schedule; they've got me in a new job."

"Kadasha, I'm working with you," Precious said, her voice firm, "but you have to work with me. I am not giving you grunt work. This is work that I need done."

"Precious, I know, I know," Kadasha admitted. "I'm sorry. I'm going to try."

"Alright," Precious said. "Just let me know. I will work with you because I do not want you to lose your job. I worked at the housing authority, and I know the chaos at that organization."

"Okay, you're right," Kadasha answered. "I understand that I've let you down. I'm going to try to do better."

"I'm working with you here," Precious emphasized, "but you have to work with me. I need this work done."

## ANTICIPATING THE SECOND FIELD LIAISON VISIT

Mr. Swann was scheduled for a second visit to Action, Inc., near the end of November. Thinking ahead to their meeting, Precious could not decide what or how much to tell him about Kadasha. Although Precious had talked to her several times about her work, Kadasha was still not consistently showing up for her internship. She was missing deadlines, and she submitted work that was riddled with mistakes, which required Precious to make extensive edits. *I care about her*, Precious reminded herself, *and I don't want to keep her from graduating. I understand why she's struggling. What am I gonna say? I can't sell her out. I don't want to make it any more difficult for her. I'm afraid if she doesn't do well with me, they're gonna put her somewhere else*, Precious reasoned. *She's been through so much. I know other students who struggled at her previous internship, and I also understand the pressure at the housing authority. Honestly, I think she wants to do well, and I know she's not really good. I know she's also struggling with her schoolwork. It feels wrong to dump any more on her.*

# 2

## TRIGGERS . . . TRIGGERS . . .

*Tamara Estes Savage, Terry A. Wolfer, and Melissa C. Reitmeier*

Field instructor Bob York was perplexed by the reaction of Miguel Taddeo, an advanced-year field student, to a client during an intake interview. Miguel was usually attentive, well prepared, and inquisitive. His internship had begun with such promise, but that day in mid-September, he seemed disengaged and distant. When they returned to Bob's office to process the interview, Bob asked Miguel about his apparent withdrawal.

"The interview bothered me," Miguel said with a shrug as he shifted in his seat.

"Oh, okay. So why did the interview bother you?" Bob probed.

---

This decision case was prepared solely to provide material for class discussion and not to suggest either effective or ineffective handling of the situation depicted. While based on field research regarding an actual situation, names and certain facts may have been disguised to protect confidentiality. The authors wish to thank the case reporter for cooperation in making this account available for the benefit of social work students and practitioners.

Miguel paused, looked at Bob, and took a deep breath. "The client looks like one of my childhood friends. He committed suicide when we were in high school."

Taken aback, Bob's first thought was, *Oh, dear. This could get deep.* "I'm sure it's hard," Bob offered tentatively, "working with people who remind you of stuff that's happened in your life."

"Yeah," Miguel stated abruptly, "but I don't think I can handle working with kids if they're going to be like that."

"Like what?" Bob asked, confused.

"If they are going to be like my friend. It isn't the kind of trouble he got into or anything like that," Miguel explained. "I mean, he was way too much like my friend, and that really froze me when we were talking."

"Sometimes this kind of thing happens when someone reminds us of someone we knew," Bob continued. "That's really a normal reaction."

"Oh, I'm sure it is," Miguel rejoined dismissively. "I'm sure other people have had the same experiences and feelings that I do, but still . . ."

"But still what?" Bob asked.

"He was just too much like my friend," Miguel insisted.

## TREE HOUSE OF TALLAHASSEE

Tree House of Tallahassee, a therapeutic group home, was established in 1986 in Tallahassee, Florida. It provided a continuum of clinical services and placement settings, including temporary out-of-home placements for boys and girls aged eight to sixteen who had behavioral problems and conflicts with caregivers that prevented them from living at home. Upon arrival, children were placed in either the low-management cottage or one of the moderate-management cottages. The low-management cottage had room for up to eighteen children who were aged fourteen and older. It housed both boys and girls, with boys on one side of the cottage and girls on the other. There were three moderate-management cottages, two cottages of boys and one cottage of girls, each with room for up to twelve children. The two boys' cottages were segregated by age, with boys aged eight to thirteen in one and boys aged fourteen to sixteen in the other. The children attended local schools unless they were behind academically, in which case they were taught at Tree House until ready for public school.

## BOB YORK, CLINICAL CASE MANAGER

Bob York was white and twenty-seven years old and had wavy, dark hair and a wiry frame. He began his social work education at the University of Maryland. While obtaining his degree, he completed an employment-based internship at a family shelter that provided case management and crisis management services. Immediately after graduating with a BSW in 1996, Bob entered Florida State University's MSW program as an advanced-standing student. He interned at the state's Department of Juvenile Justice and was offered employment by the agency after graduating in May 1997. He worked for the department until January 1998, when he began working for Southbridge Center, a private residential center for boys with a mental health diagnosis who were incarcerated within the juvenile justice system. In addition, boys were placed at Southbridge if considered at risk for sexual abuse by peers in juvenile detention. While working at Southbridge Center, Bob also supervised human services interns. After working there for two and a half years, he left in November to work at Tree House as a clinical case manager for younger boys (aged eight to thirteen) in a moderate-management cottage.

## THE INTERVIEW

After working at Tree House for ten months, Bob decided he was ready to supervise another student intern. After completing some paperwork, Tree House was included among the field sites listed by the Florida State University Office of Field Education.

Shortly thereafter, Bob received a phone call from Miguel Taddeo, a potential intern who was interested in working with kids and reported having some experience with this population. Bob set up a preplacement interview for the following week.

When they met for the interview, Bob noted that Miguel was clean shaven and well groomed. He appeared somewhat shy—or at least reserved and guarded about personal information. Miguel stated that he was fluent in Spanish and acknowledged having a large extended family in the Tallahassee area and an older sister with whom he felt close. He mentioned that he chose to interview with Tree House because of his interest in working with children and adolescents.

"Before applying to the MSW program, I wasn't certain whether social work was the right next step for me. I only knew I wanted to work with teenagers and youth. I've had some good experience working with kids."

"So, Miguel," Bob began, "tell me about your experience."

"Well," Miguel replied, "I got experience working with at-risk middle school youth in an after-school program for my BSW placement. I also worked as a camp counselor for kids this summer. I really enjoy working with the youth, and I get along well with both the boys and the girls."

"Interesting," Bob responded. "I work primarily with the younger boys in the moderate-management cottage, and sometimes we have to deal with crisis situations. In typical crisis situations, residents fight with one another; refuse to comply with boundaries, as when they leave the facility grounds; refuse to get into a vehicle; cut school; and verbally report suicidal ideation. Do you think you could work with this population of kids?"

"I've never worked with children in a group home setting before," Miguel replied. "I mean, my supervisor at the after-school program did tell me that some of the students I worked with did live in group homes, but I did not know which students they were. So this is my first experience."

"How about working with crisis situations?" Bob asked.

"Again, I don't have any experience with that," Miguel replied, "but I'm willing to learn."

"Okay, let me explain the particulars of the agency," Bob stated. "Tree House was founded in 1986 and provides therapeutic services to the children. It's overseen by an executive director and a board of directors, but we have little to no interactions with those folks. Most children we work with are eight to sixteen years old. They come from broken families or abuse and neglect situations, and the level of involvement with Department of Social Services is high. Family members aren't involved that much, if at all. Do you have any questions so far?"

"No, I'm good," Miguel replied.

"Alright. Just chime in if you have any questions or if I'm going too quickly," Bob encouraged. "Additionally, we rely on in-house RCs [residential counselors] for twenty-four-hour supervision, and the children often receive more 'upbringing' from them than from us, the clinicians. So it's important for us to develop strong relationships with the RCs. However, this can be difficult because we have more turnover among the RCs than the children. So, knowing all of that, do you think you are interested in doing an internship here?"

"I am," Miguel replied eagerly. "I would like to do my internship here."

"Great!" Bob affirmed. "I think you'll be a good fit with our organization and you'll have a good learning experience with us."

"Yeah," Miguel added, "this is something I will be comfortable doing."

## THE INTERNSHIP

On August 15, Miguel began the internship. At the outset, he primarily shadowed Bob during admission and discharge interviews. Miguel watched closely during these interviews and took notes in a notebook he carried everywhere. In supervision sessions, he asked questions and answered Bob's questions with confidence. He remembered clients' names and engaged in small talk with them. During the first two weeks, he continued to shadow Bob and take notes, but Bob noticed he would venture into something new only when prompted. As time passed, Miguel began staying in the office to read the policy manual instead of engaging in other activities. Bob offered him opportunities to attend new assessments, client sessions, and discharges, but Miguel said he did not want to see that; instead, he wanted to read more about policy. By mid-September, Bob had to insist that Miguel accompany him to assess a new client. He agreed, but Bob noticed that his facial features and body appeared to tighten and he became quiet.

The assessment was with Chase Saunders, a nine-year-old boy who had arrived at Tree House the previous night. Bob introduced himself and Miguel. Miguel greeted Chase, shook his hand, and took a seat. Miguel placed his notebook on his lap, along with a blank assessment form. Bob began the assessment by asking Chase about his history. As the client began talking about his family and the strife that led to his placement at Tree House, Bob noticed that Miguel was no longer making eye contact with the client but was looking down at the floor. The boy had lived in several foster placements and another group home. As he continued to talk about his life, Bob noticed that Miguel was taking few notes. Chase was more talkative than most clients and provided a lot of information. But as Bob continued to gather information about his history, Miguel completely stopped taking notes. Bob also noticed that Miguel was sitting up very straight with his hands in his lap. Throughout the remainder of the interview, Miguel continued to stare at the floor, shifting his gaze only to look at his watch once or twice. Toward the end of the interview, Bob attempted to involve Miguel.

"Miguel, do you have any questions that you would like to ask?" Bob asked.

"No, I understand what you are saying," Miguel replied.

"Um, alright," Bob replied.

## DEBRIEFING

After Bob concluded the assessment, he and Miguel returned to Bob's office to discuss the case.

"What did you think about the client's responses?" Bob asked.

"Oh, they seemed fine," Miguel replied distractedly.

"Okay," Bob stated.

Miguel was not making any eye contact. He still had his head down. He was looking at the incomplete assessment form, but because he had written so few notes on it during the assessment, Bob wondered, *What are you looking at?*

"So I noticed that you didn't write much today," Bob stated.

"Yes," Miguel replied.

"Are you getting more comfortable with the process?" Bob inquired.

"No," Miguel replied curtly. "I was bothered by it." For the first time since the assessment interview, Miguel looked at Bob.

"How so?" Bob inquired, surprised.

"The interview bothered me," Miguel said with a shrug as he shifted in his seat.

"Oh, okay. So why did the interview bother you?" Bob probed.

Miguel paused, looked at Bob, and took a deep breath. "Chase looks like one of my childhood friends. He committed suicide when we were in high school."

Taken aback, Bob didn't know what to say. His first thought was, *Oh, dear. This could get deep. I hope he doesn't cry. Please do NOT cry.* Finally, he asked, "How long were you friends?"

"Since elementary school," Miguel remembered.

"So Chase looks like your friend?" Bob inquired.

"Yeah," Miguel replied, "yeah, he does."

"Oh. Is there anything other than his physical appearance," Bob probed, "that reminds you of your friend?"

"There is something else," Miguel answered, "but I can't figure it out."

"Oh, I see," Bob murmured. *I really do not want to do therapy with Miguel, and I do not want him to cry! I wish he was okay and would just move on—let it go—like magic.* Then he offered, "You know this was just one assessment, and it does not mean that you will be working with the client a lot."

"Okay," Miguel replied, his voice wavering.

"Of course, we can talk about it more," Bob offered, "if you want."

"No," Miguel replied, regaining his composure.

"Alright," Bob responded, "but during our next supervision meeting, I am going to ask you about it again. Okay?"

"Okay," Miguel agreed.

## CONTACTING THE FIELD LIAISON

Bob decided to call Jack Brown, a retired social worker employed as a field liaison by the Office of Field Education. His job was to act as a bridge connecting the student, the field organization, and the office. A veteran social worker and liaison, Jack managed about twenty placements per year. He was older, walked with a cane, and was typically slow to respond to requests from field placements. But when he was present, he was great. In addition, he preferred to set up face-to-face meetings rather than talk on the phone. He would often say to Bob, "How about we set up a time to talk in person and we can have lunch? When can you meet this week?" It sometimes annoyed Bob because

Jack never asked what the concern was. He would just want to meet first before discussing any issues.

Bracing for this, Bob unfortunately reached Jack's voice mail and left a message: "Hi, this is Bob. I have a question about Miguel." *I should not leave too much information on the phone, and I don't know what kind of support I actually need.* "Um. Can you call me as soon as possible?"

## THE NEXT SUPERVISION

Bob had not yet heard from Jack when Miguel arrived for their regularly scheduled weekly supervision session the following day. Bob began with some general questions about how Miguel was progressing in his internship before commenting, "I noticed you saw Chase and exchanged hellos earlier today."

"Yeah," Miguel replied.

"So how are you doing?" Bob asked.

"Alright," Miguel said.

"I'm sure it's hard," Bob offered tentatively, "working with people who remind you of stuff that's happened in your life."

"Yeah," Miguel stated abruptly, "but I don't think I can handle working with kids if they're going to be like that."

"Like what?" Bob asked, confused.

"If they are going to be like my friend. It isn't the kind of trouble he got into or anything like that," Miguel explained. "I mean, he was way too much like my friend, and that really froze me when we were talking."

"Sometimes this kind of thing happens when someone reminds us of someone we knew," Bob continued. "That's really a normal reaction."

"Oh, I'm sure it is," Miguel rejoined dismissively. "I'm sure other people have had the same experiences and feelings that I do, but still . . ."

"But still what?" Bob asked.

"He was just too much like my friend," Miguel insisted.

# 3

# SLIPPERY BOUNDARIES

*Tamara Estes Savage, Terry A. Wolfer, and Melissa C. Reitmeier*

"I'm just wondering if you're enjoying your placement," ventured Justine Reinelt.

"Yes, I am," confirmed Latisha Norwood.

It was mid-September, one month after Latisha's social work internship began, and she and Justine, her field instructor, were nearing the end of their regular weekly supervision session. "I'm wondering," Justine tried to explain, "because you sigh a lot when you come into the office in the morning. And you sigh over and over, even on the floor. Is everything alright?"

---

This decision case was prepared solely to provide material for class discussion and not to suggest either effective or ineffective handling of the situation depicted. While based on field research regarding an actual situation, names and certain facts may have been disguised to protect confidentiality. The authors wish to thank the case reporter for cooperation in making this account available for the benefit of social work students and practitioners.

"Yes," Latisha bristled. "I have a lot going on in my life. I am fine. You know what—to be perfectly honest, you were really condescending when you told me that I needed to enjoy my time as a student."

Taken aback, Justine asked, "Can you please clarify?"

"You don't know what goes on in my life," Latisha insisted. "You don't know what kind of financial pressures I'm under. I have a mortgage. There's a lot going on in my life, so I need the part-time jobs."

"I was only trying to give feedback," Justine explained. "You told me that you quit your full-time job to focus on school, so it seemed contradictory that you would then take four part-time jobs. You are right—it *is* your decision. I'm just worried that you're spreading yourself too thin when you have all these jobs while pursuing a dual degree, completing a big project, and taking on a social work internship. That's a lot."

"You are right," Latisha retorted. "It is *my* decision, and I don't appreciate your comments."

Suddenly, supervising an intern did not seem so rewarding to Justine, and May was a long way off.

## UNIVERSITY OF NORTH CAROLINA HOSPITALS

University of North Carolina (UNC) Hospitals was founded in 1952 in Chapel Hill. With 803 beds, it had become one of the largest hospitals in North Carolina and served patients from throughout the state. UNC Hospitals was also a teaching facility affiliated with UNC and thus provided training opportunities for its students in the health care professions. In addition to medical personnel, the hospital had a large staff of social workers, with one social worker assigned to each of its fifteen units. As part of the social work department, the unit social workers were directly supervised by the social work manager, and she was supervised by the director of case management, a nurse.

## JUSTINE REINELT, SOCIAL WORK CASE MANAGER

Justine Reinelt was white and grew up in Mebane, North Carolina, a small town about one hour northwest of Chapel Hill. She graduated from North Carolina State University in 2005 with a degree in psychology. She was contemplating a career as a Christian counselor when a man at her grandmother's church advised her to get an MSW. She took his advice and applied to the MSW program at UNC at Chapel Hill. After her first field placement in the adolescent psychiatric unit at Holly Hills Hospital, Justine realized she did not want to pursue counseling. She did not enjoy group therapy or working with adolescents.

Her second field placement was at Protection and Advocacy for People with Disabilities (P&A) in Raleigh, North Carolina. This was a macro-level placement, and Justine enjoyed the work. She completed the internship, graduated in May 2007, and immediately accepted a position at P&A as a traumatic brain injury advocate. After a year, however, she realized that she and her supervisor, a lawyer, practiced from two vastly different perspectives. Justine did not think she was getting the social work supervision she needed to grow professionally and left P&A to take a position at UNC Hospitals in October 2008.

As a social work case manager, Justine was responsible for a general medical unit comprised of thirty beds. Its diverse patient population presented with a variety of medical conditions. In addition, she worked with professionals from numerous disciplines such as doctors, nurses, physical therapists, occupational therapists, and speech therapists. She met with patients as soon as they arrived on the unit to connect them to resources and make referrals. However, her primary responsibility was discharge planning. After completing a full assessment, she focused on helping patients make a smooth transition from the hospital to their home or other care facility.

## THE DECISION

The hospital's social work department encouraged staff to serve as field instructors. The social work manager appointed Janice Brinkley, a social worker with many years of experience supervising field interns, to recruit field instructors in the department and to organize intern interviews. During Justine's first year of employment, Janice asked her about serving as a field instructor, but Justine declined because she wanted to become more acquainted with her new job before taking on that responsibility. In 2010, however, Justine agreed. She knew her unit would provide a rich learning experience for a student intern because of the diverse patient population and medical issues. Her patients tended to stay in the hospital longer than patients in other units—typically five to ten days—so weekly interns could see some patients from admission to discharge. In a large hospital, she could also encourage interns to shadow social workers in other units such as Neonatal Intensive Care, Children's Hospital, and the HIV Clinic.

The department used a four-step process to recruit student interns. First, representatives from the department gathered intern applications at the university's Field Fair, held each year in the spring. Second, they offered interviews to only those students who submitted applications and followed up to express interest. Third, they interviewed students. Finally, after the interviews, both students and social workers listed their top three choices for field instructor and intern, respectively.

Justine was especially impressed with Latisha Norwood, an African American second-year student pursuing a dual degree (MSW/MPH). Latisha was the same age as Justine. At the interview, Latisha was dressed professionally and well groomed. She made good eye contact, answered questions well, and appeared eager. *She isn't going to waste time*, Justine thought. *She's a go-getter*. It was also a plus that Latisha had field experience in substance abuse from her previous internship because many patients came to the general medical unit with substance abuse issues. Justine put Latisha at the top of her potential student interns list, and Latisha stated that she wanted to work with Justine. The decision was made.

## THE BEGINNING OF THE SEMESTER

Latisha began the internship in mid-August 2010. During the first week, Justine checked in with Latisha daily. They had supervisory meetings in the calm hospital atrium near the Starbucks at the end of the day. Justine would ask Latisha how her day went and whether she was uncomfortable with anything. Justine also asked Latisha what she had learned that day, what she hoped to improve on, what she would like help with, and if there was anything else she wanted to discuss. At the end of the first week, during supervision, Justine asked Latisha how everything was working out.

"I quit my full-time job," Latisha volunteered. "I think it's important to allow myself more time to focus on school."

"That sounds like a good plan," Justine affirmed. "Being able to really enjoy this time while you're in school is important."

Two weeks later, however, Latisha mentioned that she had obtained four part-time jobs.

"Oh." Justine sounded puzzled. "You quit your full-time job to focus on school, right? But now you decided to get four part-time jobs?"

"Yes," Latisha replied.

"I hope you enjoy this time as a student and all the experiences that come with it," Justine encouraged. Then she added, "I really wish you could just focus on school."

## THE CONFRONTATION

As Latisha continued her internship, she performed well. She was proficient with patients. She didn't seem to skim through tasks or miss things. She was efficient and generally excelled in her work. However, Justine noticed that she sighed a lot and said, "Good morning" in a flat tone. *Is she having a good time? Is she bored? Is she just tired?*

During a weekly supervisory meeting after one month in placement, Latisha raised a new issue. "Justine, I have a project that I have to do for my public health degree, and I was wondering if you could supervise it and sign off on it?"

"Tell me about it," Justine replied.

Latisha explained the project. She planned to focus on patients with the five most frequent admission diagnoses and determine whether providing more information on education and community resources would prevent subsequent readmissions for these patients. She would need to access hospital admission data and wanted Justine to help with data analysis.

"Latisha, I can't supervise you or sign off on your project," Justine demurred. "I don't have a master's in public health. I'm not qualified. I can help you find resources to help with your project, but I can't sign off on the data analysis."

"But I need someone to supervise this," Latisha stated emphatically, "and this is a social work internship. You're supposed to help me with the project."

"No," Justine insisted. "I will help you, but I won't supervise the project. It's outside my expertise. I'm a social worker, not a public health administrator. We could ask the hospital business analyst to help you with statistical questions," Justine offered, "and you could use a couple of hours a week of your internship time to work on the project."

Latisha nodded in agreement.

"Is there anything else you would like to talk about today?" Justine asked. "I'm just wondering if you're enjoying your placement."

"Yes, I am," Latisha confirmed.

"I'm just wondering," Justine tried to explain, "because you sigh a lot when you come into the office in the morning. And you sigh over and over, even on the floor. Is everything alright?"

"Yes," Latisha bristled. "I have a lot going on in my life. I am fine. You know what—to be perfectly honest, you were really condescending when you told me that I needed to enjoy my time as a student."

Taken aback, Justine asked, "Can you please clarify?"

"You don't know what goes on in my life," Latisha insisted. "You don't know what kind of financial pressures I'm under. I have a mortgage. There's a lot going on in my life, so I need the part-time jobs."

"I was only trying to give feedback," Justine explained. "You told me that you quit your full-time job to focus on school, so it seemed contradictory that you would then take four part-time jobs. You are right—it *is* your decision. I'm just worried that you're spreading yourself too thin when you have all these jobs while pursuing a dual degree, completing a big project, and taking on a social work internship. That's a lot."

"You are right," Latisha retorted. "It is *my* decision, and I don't appreciate your comments."

"Latisha," Justine offered, "I'm sorry if I offended you with my recommendation. You're a big girl, and you need to do what you want to do. We don't have to talk about this anymore if you don't want to."

"Well," Latisha replied curtly, "I don't want to talk about it anymore."

# 4

## WORKPLACE BULLY (A)

*Tamara Estes Savage, Terry A. Wolfer, and Melissa C. Reitmeier*

In spring 2010, field instructor Michelle Toomey noticed In Hye Kim, a BSW student intern, was preparing to leave Sister Care with a client file.

"Julie told me it was okay," In Hye explained, "and she runs the crisis line, and these are crisis line files."

"I don't care what Julie says or where the files come from," Michelle stated firmly. "You cannot take them out. I am your field instructor, and this is not okay."

"Okay. I thought that an okay from Julie made it alright," In Hye murmured. "I am sorry if I upset you."

---

This decision case was prepared solely to provide material for class discussion and not to suggest either effective or ineffective handling of the situation depicted. While based on field research regarding an actual situation, names and certain facts may have been disguised to protect confidentiality. The authors wish to thank the case reporter for cooperation in making this account available for the benefit of social work students and practitioners.

"I'm upset because client files should never leave the agency," Michelle said, exasperated. "There is private information in those files. Do you understand?"

"Yes," In Hye replied.

"Alright, In Hye," Michelle stated, "I just want you to remember that it is absolutely not okay to take files out of the agency."

"I am sorry." In Hye's voice began to quaver.

"It's okay," Michelle said reassuringly. "Just don't do it again."

"I feel so ashamed," In Hye admitted.

"Like I said, it's alright," Michelle explained. "No harm was done this time."

"My parents would be so ashamed if they knew that I had done this. I cannot believe . . . " In Hye's voice trailed off, and she began to cry softly.

"No . . . no, it's really alright," Michelle reiterated. "If you have questions about a procedure or anything else, instead of asking Julie, ask me because I'm your field instructor. I have to sign off on all your documents, and I need to know what you're doing."

"Of course, you are my supervisor," In Hye responded. "I should have listened to you."

*Why does Julie keep intruding? In Hye is not her student.* After In Hye left her office, Michelle pondered her next step. *Is talking with In Hye enough? Or do I need to sort this out with Julie?*

## SISTER CARE

Sister Care began in 1971 as a twenty-four-hour crisis line. In 1981, with the advent of mental health services and women's health services in Urbana-Champaign, Illinois, Sister Care staff realized there was a need for domestic violence programming. Thus, Sister Care added a Domestic Violence Shelter for women and children. In 1988, Sister Care opened a Rape Crisis Center, began providing legal advocacy services, and initiated a violence prevention program. In the early 1990s, the organization expanded, offering transitional housing to women who had experienced abuse and their children, as well as child care.

Every March the Rape Crisis Center conducted its training for hospital accompaniment volunteers. These volunteers were trained to meet with rape survivors at the hospital after they had experienced an assault. Since confidentiality was paramount at the agency, it was an integral part of the volunteer training. Furthermore, in accord with agency policy, all client files were locked in file cabinets. Thus, once social workers accessed the files, they returned them and relocked the cabinets. Client files were never taken out of the organization, even if all identifying information was redacted with a permanent marker.

## MICHELLE TOOMEY, RAPE CRISIS CENTER DIRECTOR

Michelle Toomey, a white woman, had a long history with Sister Care. Her favorite aunt began working at the Domestic Violence Shelter when Michelle was in grade school and introduced her to the facility. Sometimes, when her mother was out of town, Michelle spent after-school time at the shelter with this aunt. Later, as a college student at the University of Illinois, she ran the violence prevention program. The program was designed to prevent dating, domestic, and sexual violence and was offered to middle and high schools and youth programs in the Urbana-Champaign area. She graduated with her BSW in 2005 and continued to manage the program until she left to pursue her MSW at the University of Houston. When she received her MSW in July 2008, she was forty weeks pregnant. Her daughter was born the next week, and she moved back to Urbana three weeks later. However, she had difficulty finding a job because the national economic recession resulted in hiring freezes throughout Urbana-Champaign. She worked temporary jobs until her "dream job" as the director of the Rape Crisis Center at Sister Care became available in March 2009.

As director of the Rape Crisis Center, Michelle was frequently on call twenty-four hours a day/seven days a week while also taking care of her baby. By July, she realized that she needed help. Because the agency could not hire another social worker, she thought of serving as a field instructor for a student intern. She knew she could provide a rich learning experience for a student because she had so much experience working for the agency and had focused on trauma and abuse for her entire career.

## JULIE JORDAN, DOMESTIC VIOLENCE SHELTER CASE MANAGER/CRISIS LINE DIRECTOR

Julie Jordan was white, the same age as Michelle, and the single mother of a young child. Julie had worked at the Domestic Violence Shelter since Michelle had run the violence prevention program in college. She had begun work on her MSW at University of Illinois but left the program after one semester. So far as Michelle knew, Julie did not have family or friends for support. Personally, Michelle had tried to develop a friendship with Julie, making her cookies and occasionally meeting her after work for dinner. She enjoyed Julie's company, but Julie wanted to spend more time with her than she was able to give because she was too busy with her family. There was never an argument, but Julie no longer asked Michelle to dinner or called her to talk. Michelle never spoke to Julie about it until colleagues at Sister Care told her that Julie was posting notes about her on Facebook. When Michelle asked her about the posts, Julie replied that the posts were not about Michelle. Professionally, Michelle was concerned about Julie's practice of banning clients for "life" if they went back to their abusers. Michelle suspected that Julie had sometimes kicked clients out of the Domestic Violence Shelter because she did not like them. Even though Michelle had many concerns about Julie, the two women had coexisted professionally.

## THE INTERVIEW

Michelle called the School of Social Work at the University of Illinois and requested a BSW intern. It was July, late in the internship placement process. However, the program had not yet placed one second-year BSW student, In Hye Kim, who was twenty-two years old. She was born in Korea and had spent the first thirteen years of her life there before moving to the United States with her family. Thus, English was her second language.

After a brief phone conversation, Michelle and In Hye agreed to an interview at the Rape Crisis Center. Michelle met In Hye in the lobby of the center.

"Hello, In Hye. I'm Michelle Toomey."

"Hi," replied In Hye. "Nice to meet you."

"Nice to meet you, too," Michelle said. "Did you have trouble finding the center?"

"No," In Hye replied. "Your directions were great! Urbana-Champaign is so large and confusing, but your directions were very clear."

"Wonderful!" Michelle stated enthusiastically. "Let's go to my office and discuss the internship, okay?"

"Okay. Sounds good," In Hye replied.

"Have a seat, In Hye." Michelle gestured to the chair in front of her desk. "Now let me tell you a bit about the organization."

"Oh, I know about some of the services," In Hye interjected.

"You do? Wonderful," Michelle replied. "Tell me what you know."

"Well," In Hye continued, "Sister Care has been around since 1971 and there are many programs."

"Yes," Michelle nodded.

"Yes," In Hye continued, "and you offer a crisis line, the Domestic Violence Shelter, transitional housing, and the Rape Crisis Center."

"Very good!" Michelle was impressed.

"Thank you," In Hye blushed. "I studied the website so that I would be prepared for the interview. I always like to be prepared. I am excited for this opportunity."

"Well, In Hye, I am excited, too," Michelle responded. "If you accept the placement, you will be working with me at the Rape Crisis Center. We provide training to volunteers, plan fund-raising events, write grants, and provide crisis intervention for rape victims at the hospital. Of course, you would be involved with the crisis intervention only if you feel comfortable. It's not a requirement for the internship. I've said a lot," Michelle paused. "Do you have any questions?"

"Yes," In Hye answered. "Will I have an opportunity to become involved with the other programs? I am interested in the crisis line."

"Yes," Michelle replied. "Of course, you can structure your internship in a way that best fits your learning needs and interests. However, I will need you in the Rape Crisis Center for the majority of your internship time."

"Okay," In Hye agreed.

"Have you had any experience working with rape victims or survivors of domestic violence?" Michelle asked.

"No," In Hye explained, "but I'm interested in working with victims of violence in the future."

"Alright," Michelle said. "Then this placement will be a nice start in that direction. How does this sound to you? Do you have any questions?"

"It sounds fine," In Hye answered. "So I won't have to be on call to go to the hospital to help a rape victim?"

"Only if you want to," Michelle assured her. "It's completely up to you. If you decide you are interested, there is training in the spring. Anything else?"

"No . . . I mean yes," In Hye stammered. "I'm sorry. There is one more thing, and I hope it won't be a problem because I really want this internship. My dad abused my mom when I was a child, so I grew up seeing that. Will that keep me from getting the internship?"

"Of course not, In Hye. I'm sorry that happened," Michelle replied. "Thank you for sharing that. No, it won't keep you from doing your internship here, but we will need to make sure you are emotionally alright throughout the internship. Your experiences here may trigger memories and you might need help with that. I need you to be honest with me if you are ever uncomfortable or think you need help, alright?"

"Alright," In Hye replied. "I think this practicum would be very helpful for me given my past experiences."

*Now I'm a bit concerned*, Michelle realized. *I don't think this will be a problem. I'll just take it slowly with her when it comes to direct service.* "Okay," Michelle said. "We will take things slowly, and you let me know if you are uncomfortable or need more time to process anything that concerns you. How does that sound?"

"That sounds great!" In Hye replied. "I am really excited about this opportunity."

"One more thing," Michelle added. "Our clients must receive absolute confidentiality. So I need to ask that you not discuss or pass any information about our clients or their situations outside of this agency. Do you understand the need for that stipulation?"

"Oh, absolutely," In Hye said, nodding her agreement. "I wouldn't expect anything less."

*I know she will have challenges with direct service*, Michelle reassured herself after In Hye left, *but she's really smart. She also seems to be on the ball with organizational tasks. Plus she's really sweet. I think this is going to work out fine.*

Once the semester began, Michelle made sure that In Hye attended the necessary trainings so that she was fully oriented to the agency's programs. In Hye also spent time at the Rape Crisis Center, the Domestic Violence Shelter, and the crisis line office. While at the crisis line, In Hye was trained by Julie. Michelle noticed that In Hye and Julie usually went out to lunch together when In Hye worked on the crisis line. In Hye once asked Michelle if she was on Facebook. When Michelle told her she wasn't, In Hye mentioned that she was Facebook friends with Julie. Michelle also noticed that In Hye would often cite Julie's perspective on organizational issues, such as "Well, Julie thinks . . ." or "Julie said . . . ." But Michelle had no concerns because In Hye was meeting all the expectations of the internship; she was reliable, conscientious, and responsive to supervision. Given her own past relationship with Julie, however, Michelle was concerned about In Hye's apparent closeness to Julie.

Then Christmas neared. The agency had a holiday on-call rotation calendar, which Julie managed, to ensure that on-call duties were equally distributed among the staff. Because Michelle volunteered for on-call duty over the Thanksgiving holiday, she was surprised when Julie assigned her on-call duty for the week of Christmas, and she decided to approach Julie about it.

"Julie," Michelle began, "I think there is a mistake with the on-call calendar."

"What kind of mistake?" Julie asked.

"Well," Michelle replied, "I'm on call for the Christmas holiday, and I was just on call for the Thanksgiving holiday. Plus, even if you didn't take into account that I covered the last major holiday, we rotate every seven weeks. It hasn't been seven weeks since Thanksgiving."

"That is not a mistake, Michelle," Julie stated.

"What do you mean?" Michelle asked. "It isn't fair. That doesn't make sense. Why do I have to cover two holidays back to back, especially since it isn't my time in the rotation?"

"Well, I'm sorry," Julie responded.

"Listen, I will take any other holiday, but I need Christmas off," Michelle insisted.

"Sorry, the new girl always gets it," Julie replied. "It is just how we do things."

"Julie, that is not true," Michelle retorted. "That is not the policy. We rotate the on-call duties among us fairly."

"Michelle, I'm sorry," Julie repeated, "but that is how the calendar works."

When Michelle appealed to the agency's executive director, she volunteered to take on-call duty over the Christmas holidays herself.

## THE INTERNSHIP: SECOND SEMESTER

In January, Michelle became concerned during a supervisory meeting when she noticed that In Hye had a client file in her school binder.

"In Hye, are you adding case notes to that client file?" Michelle asked, gesturing to the file.

"Oh, no," In Hye answered. "I need a sample file for a school assignment. Julie told me I could just use a client file instead of making one up. She said it would save me time since all these files are available."

"In Hye, I told you that you cannot take client files out of the shelter," Michelle replied, astonished.

"Well, Julie told me it was okay. I emailed her and asked her," In Hye stated. "Plus I covered up the client's name on the folder and throughout the file."

"Okay." Michelle paused. "First of all, when you cover up client names and identifying information, you have to use a permanent marker, not a regular marker, because I can see the name coming through."

"Oh," In Hye murmured.

"Second of all," Michelle asked, "why did you email Julie instead of me? I already told you that you absolutely could not do that. It's just not safe to take files out of the agency."

"But she told me it was okay, and she runs the crisis line, and these are crisis line files," In Hye explained.

"I don't care what Julie says or where the files come from," Michelle stated firmly. "You cannot take them out. I am your field instructor, and this is not okay."

"Okay. I thought that an okay from Julie made it alright," In Hye murmured. "I am sorry if I upset you."

"I'm upset because client files should never leave the agency," Michelle said, exasperated. "There is private information in those files. Do you understand?"

"Yes," In Hye replied.

"Alright, In Hye," Michelle stated, "I just want you to remember that it is absolutely not okay to take files out of the agency."

"I am sorry." In Hye's voice began to quaver.

"It's okay," Michelle said reassuringly. "Just don't do it again."

"I feel so ashamed," In Hye admitted.

"Like I said, it's alright," Michelle explained. "No harm was done this time."

"My parents would be so ashamed if they knew that I had done this. I cannot believe . . . " In Hye's voice trailed off, and she began to cry softly.

"No . . . no, it's really alright," Michelle reiterated. "If you have questions about a procedure or anything else, instead of asking Julie, ask me because I'm your field instructor. I have to sign off on all your documents, and I need to know what you're doing."

"Of course, you are my supervisor," In Hye responded. "I should have listened to you."

*Why does Julie keep intruding? In Hye is not her student.* After In Hye left, Michelle pondered her next step. *Is talking with In Hye enough? Or do I need to sort this out with Julie?*

# 5

## IS HE OKAY?

*Robert Jay Palmer, Terry A. Wolfer, and Melissa C. Reitmeier*

Glovanna Claypool, Mather Middle School's social worker, had just finished an afternoon phone call with Big Brothers Big Sisters when she looked up and saw English teacher Dorthea Branton at her door.

"Hi, Glovanna. What's going on with Kendrick? I can hear him coughing all the way down the hall. It sounds like he's going to explode! Is he okay?"

"I'm not sure," Glovanna responded. "He does sound pretty bad. I just can't figure out what's going on with him. I'm sorry if his coughing is bothering the staff. I'll check on him and let you know. Thank you for your concern, Dorothea."

---

This decision case was prepared solely to provide material for class discussion and not to suggest either effective or ineffective handling of the situation depicted. While based on field research regarding an actual situation, names and certain facts may have been disguised to protect confidentiality. The authors wish to thank the case reporter for cooperation in making this account available for the benefit of social work students and practitioners.

As Glovanna stood up and headed toward the interns' office, she asked herself, *What am I going to do with that boy? He's not getting better, and now it's affecting the staff. What is my next step?*

## MATHERS MIDDLE SCHOOL

Mathers Middle School was part of the Little Rock (Arkansas) School District and enrolled sixth- through eighth-grade students. It had just moved to the newly renovated campus of the old Royale High School, an icon to members of the local community. Although the property had been newly remodeled for the middle school, the two-story brick building kept most of its original architecture and charm with outdoor hallways, a large central courtyard, and eighty-year-old magnolia trees. Mathers's student body of 395 was much smaller than that of Royale, so it occupied only a portion of the property. The unoccupied parts of the campus were still being renovated for other purposes.

Many of the families in the community served by Mathers had resided in their neighborhoods for multiple generations. Reflecting the demographic makeup of the surrounding neighborhoods, approximately 95 percent of the students were African American. Around 85 percent of the students qualified for free lunch. The previous year the Little Rock School District had designated Mathers Middle School a "priority school." Priority schools were given additional school district funds and other resources because their students did not perform well on state achievement tests. The staff at Mathers had ambivalent feelings about the designation. It meant that they had additional resources from the district, such as a full-time social worker, but it also meant that they were subject to additional scrutiny and reporting requirements, which made for a high-pressure environment.

## GLOVANNA CLAYPOOL, SCHOOL SOCIAL WORKER

Originally from Texarkana, Arkansas, Glovanna Claypool was an African American who moved to New York City as a child. A talented dancer, she attended the New York School for the Performing Arts. During high school, she offered free dance lessons at an inner-city school and, through this experience, developed a passion for working with economically disadvantaged youth. Wanting to help children in a more direct way, she turned down the opportunity to attend the Julliard School of Dance and instead chose to get her BSW from York College in 1986. After earning her MSW from Columbia University in 1988, she spent three years in New York City, working first with youth and then as a medical social worker. Wanting to be closer to her extended family and to return to the place where she spent her summers as a child, she moved back to Arkansas in 1991. Upon her return, she worked in substance abuse and mental health before joining the Little Rock School District in 1993. She was the director of a dropout prevention program at a high school prior to becoming the social worker for Mathers Middle School in 2009.

As the school social worker at Mathers, Glovanna was responsible for helping parents, students, and school staff identify barriers to student learning and develop interventions to improve student success. These interventions ranged from helping a family find the resources to pay a utility bill to running school-based support groups for children experiencing family violence.

Glovanna was passionate about her role as a social worker. She would say, "It is more than my career; it is my purpose and where I'm supposed to be." She demonstrated this passion by, for example, starting a nonprofit agency to serve the homeless and volunteering as an off-site field instructor. She was a strong advocate for children and was particularly drawn to working with young African American women. She frequently served as a mentor for former female students once they graduated high school. A seasoned field instructor, Glovanna had supervised well over fifty BSW and MSW students over the course of her career. She had worked with many challenging students over the years and was comfortable addressing difficult student situations. As a result, she was sometimes asked to supervise "high need students."

## INTERVIEWING KENDRICK WILSON

In spring 2009, Glovanna agreed to take two MSW field interns for the next academic year. Because of the nature of the contact between interns and middle school students, she selected her interns carefully. It was her policy to have an in-depth, face-to-face interview with each potential intern in order to assess their appropriateness for the school setting. She was on her way to one of those interviews.

One of the MSW students Glovanna decided to interview was Kendrick Wilson. As she entered the school's front office to meet him, she saw an African American man dressed in khakis and a white button-up shirt sitting with his hands clasped in front of him. He wore his hair in neatly manicured dreadlock twists and appeared to be in his early to midtwenties. Before introducing herself, Glovanna thought, *I wonder where he's from. Most guys around here don't wear dreads like those.*

"Hello, you must be Kendrick," Glovanna ventured.

"Yes, hello," Kendrick responded as he stood to greet her. "Kendrick Wilson, ma'am."

"I'm Glovanna Claypool," she said, shaking his hand. "Let's go back to my office to talk."

As they walked down the outside corridor to her office, Glovanna began explaining the layout and administrative structure of the school, using the offices they passed as points of reference. When they reached her office, she invited Kendrick to sit down and said, "So, Kendrick, tell me a little about yourself and why you're interested in doing an internship with us?"

"Well, Ms. Claypool, I'm starting in the MSW program this fall. I have a bachelor's degree in social work from the Southern Arkansas University. That is where I'm from, Magnolia."

"Sure, I've been there. That's a really small community."

"Yes, ma'am, it sure is. A lot different from here. Anyway, I'm really interested in working with children. I did my undergraduate internship at an after-school program and really liked it. I know that I want to work with kids in some capacity."

"What happened there that showed you that you want to work with kids?" Glovanna inquired.

"I think that the kids, especially the boys, looked up to me, and I knew I could be a good role model and make a difference in their lives," Kendrick answered.

As they spoke about Kendrick and his interests, Glovanna thought, *You'll be a good fit for the school.* As the interview came to an end, Glovanna said, "I've enjoyed talking with you, Kendrick. You present yourself very well. I think you would be an asset to the students here, and I hope you decide to do your internship with us."

"Thank you for giving me this opportunity, Ms. Claypool. I would like that," Kendrick stated as he stood up and shook Glovanna's hand.

As Kendrick walked out of the office, Glovanna thought, *I hope this works out. He seems a little shy and nervous, but he is very idealistic, and it would be nice to have a young black man to mentor some of the boys here.*

## WEEK ONE: ALL IS WELL

On the first day of the placement, Glovanna stepped into the office housing the two new MSW interns.

"Hi, Kendrick and Chandra. Welcome to your first day at Mathers Middle School. I'm glad you picked us as your placement site."

As she usually did, Glovanna began by giving an overview of the internship and reviewing the information she had provided during the initial interview. "I want to start by explaining to you my approach to having interns. I think of the placement as a three-phase process. The first phase is orientation. I want you to get to know the needs and resources in the neighborhoods that these kids are coming from and to get to know the program and what we do here. I want you to get to know the staff who we will be working with to help these kids, and since you will be working so closely together, I want you to get to know each other. For the second phase, you will do a lot of observation to see how we do our work and begin to establish a caseload. In phase three, you will be working with children under my supervision."

They spent the rest of the morning going over topics such as the school's policies and procedures regarding mandatory reporting, aggressive children, and intruder safety. Chandra Pederson, the second MSW intern, asked several questions about the various policies. Kendrick was attentive but said little during the meeting. Glovanna took the two interns to lunch in the afternoon. Afterward she walked them through the school and introduced them to the staff.

On Thursday, the interns began their day observing teachers in two classrooms. Like the previous day, Glovanna took them to lunch. They spent the afternoon touring the neighborhood surrounding Mathers.

## WEEK TWO: HE IS NOT FEELING WELL

At nine A.M. on Wednesday, the second field day of week two, Glovanna met with the interns to plan their activities for the day. She sat down on a wooden chair in the corner of the office so she could look at both Kendrick and Chandra without having to turn her head.

She noticed that Kendrick was rubbing his eyes while sitting in a slumped posture. Seeing that his eyes were red and that he appeared tired and distracted, she asked, "Are you feeling okay?"

"Yes, I'm okay," Kendrick assured her.

"You don't look like you are feeling very well."

"I think I have a little cold," Kendrick responded.

"Are you taking anything?" Glovanna asked.

"No," Kendrick said. "I don't like to take stuff if I don't have to."

"I understand," replied Glovanna. "I hope you can get some rest and take care of yourself."

"Thank you, Ms. Claypool. I'll be fine by next Monday," Kendrick said meekly.

The two interns worked in the office for the rest of the day. Chandra was as animated as usual and Kendrick as reserved. Glovanna noticed that Kendrick seemed a bit more tired and less focused than he had been the week before but chalked it up to his cold.

## WEEK THREE: SICK AGAIN

The next Wednesday, Kendrick came to Mathers and stopped by Glovanna's office.

"Good morning, Ms. Claypool."

"Good morning, Kendrick. How are you feeling?" Glovanna asked.

"I'm feeling much better, thank you."

"Good. I'll be in to see you and Chandra in a few minutes to talk about what you all are going to be doing this week." As Kendrick left her office, Glovanna thought, *I'm glad he's gotten better.*

Glovanna had the interns interview a teacher to gain their perspective on the children's needs and speak with representatives of the most frequently used resources in the neighborhood. On Thursday, after an early morning consultation meeting with Mathers's principal and guidance counselor, Glovanna stopped in to see the interns. As she sat down, she mused, *Kendrick's color seems off, and he looks a little disheveled. That's not like him. I hope I'm not seeing a pattern develop.*

"Wow, Kendrick, are you sick again?" Glovanna asked incredulously.

"I don't know what it is, Ms. Claypool," Kendrick said as he nodded yes.

"A couple of our staff are sick," Glovanna replied. "So maybe you caught something here. Let's see how you are doing after the weekend."

That afternoon Kendrick and Chandra prepared for their upcoming observations by reviewing the files of the children with whom Glovanna would be working. This would be the first step in giving both interns their own cases. Glovanna thought that Kendrick looked tired, but he made it through the rest of the day.

## WEEK FOUR: THE FEVER

Glovanna came into the office to discuss the agenda for the day with Kendrick and Chandra. As she started to speak, she looked at Kendrick and halted. "Kendrick, how are you feeling? You don't look very good." *You're all sweaty, breathing fast. What's going on with you?* Glovanna wondered silently.

"I don't feel all that well," Kendrick admitted.

"The school nurse is here today. Let's go and see her and get her opinion." As they walked down the hall to the nurse's office, Glovanna chose her words carefully. "You can't help kids if you're sick. And you don't want to make other people sick. What are you doing to take care of yourself?"

"I think I just have a lot going on," Kendrick responded, "with all of my class assignments and getting used to being here in Little Rock. I don't really like to take medicine, and going to the doctor costs a lot of money. I think I just need some time to catch up is all."

"They have doctors at the University Health Clinic," Glovanna said. "You can go see one of them. All the students can."

"Thank you for being concerned, Ms. Claypool, but I'll be fine. I know it."

When they arrived at the school nurse's office, the nurse, Wanda Onyango, was on the phone talking to a parent. She motioned for them to sit down as she continued her phone call. After sitting quietly for a moment, Kendrick turned to Glovanna and said, "Ms. Claypool, I know you are just about to give me these two cases and Chandra has a couple of cases." Kendrick turned his gaze to the ground in front of him as he said, "I want to do a good job here and do right by these kids. I'm afraid that if I miss too many days, I'll get behind. I know I'll shake it off soon."

"Kendrick," Glovanna continued, "I know that doing well here is important to you, and I know that you want to complete your hours so you can move forward with your education and your social work career, but your health has to come first. We can always find ways for you to make up the hours, so don't worry about that."

Wanda hung up the phone and said, "Well, good afternoon, Ms. Claypool." She nodded toward Kendrick and then continued, "I'm sorry that you had to wait. What can I do for you?"

Glovanna waited for a moment for Kendrick to answer and then took the lead.

"Kendrick here has been sick on and off since he got here a few weeks ago, but I think he's worse today. Can you look at him?"

"You look a little flushed," Wanda stated. She asked a couple of questions about his general health and then placed a thermometer in Kendrick's mouth. "You have a fever," she said. "Not a very high one—but a fever nonetheless. You might be infectious, so I have to recommend that you go home as a safety precaution for the kids and staff here, as well as yourself."

Glovanna shook her head in agreement and then asked, "Wanda, have you heard anything about some bug going around or problems with stuff in the air from the renovation?"

"Not that has come to my attention, but that doesn't rule out anything," Wanda said as she smiled. "Sometimes I'm the last to know."

As they returned to the intern office so Kendrick could pick up his belongings, Glovanna said, "Kendrick, whatever bug or flu you have, you have to get treated. If you are not taking anything, you are going to get really sick!"

"This time I'm going to take something, Ms. Claypool. I promise," Kendrick assured her.

"Be sure that you do," she admonished, trying not to sound too maternal.

After walking Kendrick out, Glovanna had a few moments before she needed to start preparing for the afternoon girls' group. She thought about many of the more challenging students she had supervised over the last twenty years. *I wonder why Kendrick keeps getting so sick. I know he is not using it as an excuse because he comes even when he's sick and he's worried about getting all of his hours done. I can't understand why he comes here, gets sick, goes home over the weekend, and comes back looking better but then gets sick again. I wonder what is going on.*

## WEEK FIVE: CHANDRA'S CONCERN

Glovanna was reading a report from a school psychologist regarding an aggressive student when she heard a soft knock at her office door and looked up.

"Hi, Ms. Claypool. Can I talk to you?"

"Of course, you can, Chandra. What can I do for you?"

Chandra looked sheepish. "I don't want to start anything, and I like Kendrick, but I'm worried about him. He sure has been coughing a lot, and he seems sick all the time. I asked him if he knew why he kept getting sick, but he just shrugged his shoulders and said, 'I dunno, but I'm good.' He's very nice to me, but he doesn't talk to me much. Can you give me advice on how to talk to him?"

Glovanna thought for a moment. "Some people are more private than other people, and that is okay. I think you are doing the right thing by showing your concern. Just keep being supportive. I think he'll be more talkative and open when he feels like it is the right time. Thank you for your concern, Chandra. That shows you're a true social worker."

After Chandra left, Glovanna reflected on the situation. *I wonder if he's having personal issues. Lord knows, I've seen my share of that over the years, but this looks like a medical problem. He really cares about the placement, so why isn't he going to the doctor to find out what is going on? Is there something he does not want to share with me? I'll keep trying.*

Glovanna had just finished an afternoon phone call with Big Brothers Big Sisters when she looked up and saw English teacher Dorthea Branton at her door.

"Hi, Glovanna. What is going on with Kendrick? I can hear him coughing all the way down the hall. It sounds like he's going to explode! Is he okay?"

"I'm not sure," Glovanna responded. "He does sound pretty bad. I just can't figure out what's going on with him. I'm sorry if his coughing is bothering the staff. I'll check on him and let you know. Thank you for your concern, Dorothea."

As Glovanna stood up and headed toward the interns' office, she asked herself, *What am I going to do with that boy? He's not getting better and now it's affecting the staff. What is my next step?*

# 6

## RELUCTANT SOCIAL WORKER

*Robert Jay Palmer, Terry A. Wolfer, and Melissa C. Reitmeier*

"I thought it was going to be a great thing for you to have a student," Lorena Lavigne offered apologetically to Alexis Pesek, the caseworker she supervised, "and usually it is."

"Well, it hasn't been," Alexis responded emphatically. "She's the most stressful part of my job. Around here, that's saying a lot. But I have a meeting with a guardian ad litem now, so can we talk about this more during tomorrow's supervision?"

"Of course," Lorena answered. "Let's do that. We'll figure it out then."

After Alexis left her office, Lorena wondered, almost aloud, *What do I do now? We just agreed to an action plan with Kim and the school,*

---

This decision case was prepared solely to provide material for class discussion and not to suggest either effective or ineffective handling of the situation depicted. While based on field research regarding an actual situation, names and certain facts may have been disguised to protect confidentiality. The authors wish to thank the case reporter for cooperation in making this account available for the benefit of social work students and practitioners.

*and I think we need to honor that agreement. But are we just setting her up for failure? And what about Alexis? Is it fair to ask her to continue working with Kim? She's at her wit's end, and I can't afford to antagonize her over this.*

## POPLAR BLUFF, MISSOURI

Nestled in the Ozark Foothills region of southeastern Missouri, the city of Poplar Bluff was the Butler County seat. The self-proclaimed "Gateway to the Ozarks," it had a population of seventeen thousand and was part of the Butler County Metropolitan Statistical Area, with a total population of fifty thousand. As the largest city in the county, it also served as the hub for most of the area's social services.

## OZARK ALLIANCE AND THE CHILD ADVOCACY CENTER

Located in two adjacent buildings just off Poplar Bluff's Main Street, Ozark Alliance was a private, nonprofit agency that served adults and children experiencing familial or sexual violence in the five-county Ozark Foothills region. It grew out of the 1999 merger of three organizations: the Women's Resource Center (WRC), the Children's Action Network (CAN), and the Child Advocacy Center (CAC). Two of the organizations, WRC and CAN, were well established in the community, while the third organization, CAC, was newly established in 1999 and joined Ozark Alliance that same year.

One of more than six hundred centers nationwide, the CAC served children who were sexually abused by providing them a comfortable, private, and child-friendly environment for forensic medical exams and interviews. It was part of a growing but well-established trend toward creating a more family- and child-friendly approach to child abuse investigations. The CAC was accredited by the National Children's Alliance, which required it to provide victim advocacy, offer trauma-focused mental health services, and use an interprofessional team approach to assess alleged abuse.

The CAC program staff consisted of a full-time director, a full-time child and family advocate, and a part-time intake coordinator.

Therapists from the WRC provided the mental health services, and the CAC contracted with private vendors—social workers and physicians—to provide the forensic interviews and medical exams, respectively.

The CAC was housed in a converted two-story brick house built in the early 1900s. An ornate wrap-around porch led to the main entrance, located at the back of the house to protect family anonymity. The waiting room was furnished with overstuffed couches and chairs to create a homelike ambiance.

## LORENA LAVIGNE, DIRECTOR OF THE CHILD ADVOCACY CENTER

Lorena Lavigne, a fifty-eight-year-old white woman, initially joined Ozark Alliance as the WRC's director of clinical services in 2005 and became the CAC's director in 2007. After earning a BSW from the University of South Florida in 1974 and an MSW from the University of Tennessee in 1978, Lorena had accumulated many years of direct practice experience. She started her MSW career at a faith-based group home in New York City and went on to work in mental health in Ohio, Tennessee, and Missouri. She was just over five feet tall, and her neatly cropped hair, wire-framed glasses, office attire, and calm and deliberate way of speaking conveyed a strong air of professionalism.

As director, Lorena was responsible for all the CAC's administrative functions, including staffing and grant writing and reporting, and she served as the program's community liaison. She enjoyed her position at the CAC, and one of her favorite responsibilities was recruiting and maintaining community members as part of the CAC's interprofessional team. Finding and reinforcing the common ground among members of such diverse disciplines as law enforcement, medicine, child protection, mental health, and victim advocacy was sometimes a difficult balancing act, but she enjoyed meeting that challenge to benefit the children and families they served.

During thirty years of professional experience, Lorena had honed a patient and tolerant approach to working with people. Her work with hundreds of clients, eleven supervisees, and twenty interns taught her that it was most effective to approach people from a strengths perspective. This was reflected in her supervision style. As she would sometimes say, “I’m not a micromanager. I hire people who can do the job and then let them.” She considered herself an “old-time social worker” and believed that social workers played a critical role in society. She was inspired when new social workers wanted to enter the field. Consequently, she enjoyed teaching and supervising students and had supervised over twenty field students through the years.

## ALEXIS PESEK, CHILD AND FAMILY ADVOCATE

A native of Missouri, Alexis Pesek was a white woman in her late thirties. After earning her BSW from Missouri State University in 2002 and her MSW from Hawai‘i Pacific University in 2004, she had worked for three years as a child protection worker in Hawai‘i. During this time, she became a skilled and competent child welfare worker and forensic interviewer. It was through her child welfare experience in Hawai‘i that Alexis developed a deep commitment to serving children and a passion for the CAC model. She returned to Missouri in 2007 when her husband secured a job in Poplar Bluffs.

Alexis was five feet tall, with dark red hair and a serious demeanor. She held herself and those around her to very high standards. Although quiet and not confrontational, her high expectations and skill level sometimes left other team members feeling a little intimidated.

For the past two years, Alexis had served as the child and family advocate at the CAC. As such, her primary responsibilities were to make the initial contact with the referred family, assess for risk, ensure child safety, and serve as a resource and support to the family during the investigation process. Her experience as a child welfare worker made her especially skilled at assessing child safety and responding to a family’s needs during a time of crisis. She enjoyed her current position but wanted more responsibility. She had no previous supervisory experience and wanted to add this to her professional repertoire.

## STAFF RELATIONSHIPS

The CAC staff had fostered a culture of open and assertive communication. Lorena, Alexis, and Connie Ginsberg, the contracted forensic interviewer, felt comfortable in their roles and respected the opinions and experience of the other team members. However, this took a sudden turn in 2009 when the CAC had to unexpectedly end its contract with Ginsberg for a breach of confidentiality. The sudden dismissal required that Lorena and Alexis "pinch hit" until they found someone to fill the position, and the dismissal damaged the CAC's reputation among some of its community partners. The ensuing fallout led to occasional passionate disagreements between Lorena and Alexis regarding the best way to rebuild community relationships.

## A PROSPECTIVE INTERN

Lorena regularly presented on the CAC's services during volunteer trainings for the WRC. At an April 2013 training, as Lorena was packing up after her presentation, a large young woman with shoulder-length sandy blonde hair and dressed in blue jeans and a red T-shirt approached.

"Hi, my name is Kim Powell," the woman said. "I really liked your presentation. I just got accepted into my MSW program and need an internship starting in August. I'm very interested in doing an internship at the CAC."

"Thanks for your interest," Lorena responded. "Where are you going to go to school?"

"I'm going to go to University of Missouri–St. Louis," Kim replied.

"That's a good program," Lorena nodded. "Where did you get your undergraduate degree?"

"I graduated last year from Missouri Valley College with a degree in criminal justice and sociology."

"That will be a good background for the work we do at the CAC," Lorena said as she zipped up her bag. "Please complete the volunteer application for our program, and I'll contact you after I have a chance to read it."

*Kim's a really heavy woman, maybe three hundred pounds*, Lorena reflected as they parted. *I wonder if that has caused any challenges for her.*

A week later Lorena looked over Kim's application. *This looks fine to me*, Lorena mused. *I wonder how she's doing as a volunteer for the*

*WRC. Since I have the luxury of an in-house reference, I'll just call and ask Andrea Corliss since she coordinates the volunteers.*

"I don't know if she has actually taken any crisis calls," Andrea said, "but she seems like a pleasant woman and appears very enthusiastic about her volunteer work with us. I assume she'd be a fine intern."

"I'm glad to know that," Lorena said. "I'd feel better if she had taken some crisis calls and we knew how she managed them, but I rarely get that kind of information about a student's skills before accepting them anyway. So 'no news is good news,' I guess. Thanks, Andrea."

*Well, no red flags,* Lorena thought as she hung up the phone, *and she wants to be here, so I'll set up an interview with her.*

## THE INITIAL INTERVIEW

Lorena was reading Alexis's monthly report when Kim knocked on the door. *Whoops,* Lorena thought as she invited Kim to sit down. *I hope she can sit comfortably in that armed office chair. I need to replace it with something more accommodating.*

"Nice to see you again, Kim," Lorena began. "So tell me a little about yourself." Lorena noticed that Kim seemed to hesitate a bit before she answered.

"Well," Kim began, "I grew up here in Poplar Bluff. My parents own a business here. I have worked for them part-time since I graduated high school in 1998. Like I told you before, I have a degree in criminal justice and sociology from Missouri Valley College."

"Since you're from here," Lorena replied, "it's possible that a family you know will come in for an interview. If we move forward with the placement, we'll talk about how you'll need to manage that."

"Hmm, I didn't think about that possibility," Kim replied.

"So tell me why you would like to do your internship with us," Lorena probed.

"I have an adult friend," Kim answered, "who is a survivor of child abuse. I have personally seen the effects of sexual assault and child abuse, and I want to help those affected."

"I appreciate your desire to make a difference. Social work is certainly the place to do that. Let me tell you about the placement. The work we do at the CAC is very sensitive. Families come into the center at the point of suspected abuse. The first step is the forensic interview with the child. Then there is a post-interview conference with a nonoffending caregiver.

"Wow, I'm not sure I would know how to do that," Kim observed.

"Oh, we would help you start slowly," Lorena explained. "Agency protocol is to have one family come in at a time. We keep doors locked and greet clients at the door. Once a family enters the premises, we require constant observation to protect children from adults who may coach them on what to say in the interview. Staff, often interns, engage with and occupy the child in small talk while the child is waiting to be interviewed. During the interview, someone talks with the nonoffending caregiver. For our master's-level interns, we also have them do that interview once they reach that skill level.

"That sounds good," Kim replied.

Lorena continued. "The forensic interviewer will come out and say to the child, 'Let me show you and mom and dad the talking room. This is where you will be, and I will bring you back out to them when we are done.' After she brings the child back into the interviewing room, someone checks in with the family to see how they're doing and to answer any questions they have. When families come in to see us, it's a fairly big crisis, so our job is to help people feel welcomed and to try to put people at ease."

Lorena went on to explain other intern responsibilities and expectations regarding attendance, confidentiality, professional demeanor, documentation, and use of supervision. Finally, she said, "Okay, I just gave you a brief overview of what we do here and what you would do as an intern. What questions do you have about how we do things here or about CACs in general? Oh, before you answer, I want to tell you that Alexis, the child and family advocate, will provide your day-to-day supervision and assign you things to do."

"I don't have any questions," Kim said. "I think this is exactly what I want to do. I was very interested in coming here after hearing your presentation. Now, after hearing you talk more about it, it sounds perfect."

"Okay," Lorena replied. "Then I would like to offer you an internship with us."

"Good. I'll take it," Kim responded.

## SUPERVISION WITH LORENA AND ALEXIS (AUGUST 13, 2013)

Lorena was looking forward to her weekly supervision meeting with Alexis. As she waited for Alexis to arrive, she reflected on her reasoning for assigning Alexis as Kim's task supervisor. *Having a student to supervise will make her job more enjoyable. She's been wanting more responsibility. Considering some of the conflicts we had during the "crisis," this demonstrates my confidence in her. I'm glad I can do this for her.*

Lorena smiled as Alexis sat down in the chair across from her. After talking about a forensic interview involving a familiar family, Lorena switched topics to the upcoming MSW intern. "I wanted to check in with you about Kim, our new intern. She'll be joining us soon," Lorena said. "Are you feeling ready for her?"

"I think so." Alexis said as she shrugged.

"I'm glad that we have a student for you, Alexis," Lorena added. "Supervising a student fits well with our discussions about how we can increase your responsibilities here and support your growth as a professional."

"I think it does, too," Alexis acknowledged. "I'm looking forward to it, but I'm a little nervous. I haven't supervised before, and I can be a little impatient with people sometimes."

*Don't I know that!* Lorena thought, but she said, "I'm sure you'll be a great supervisor."

"You told me to determine what I want an intern to know by the end of the year," Alexis continued, "and then create assignments that help her get there."

"Right," Lorena encouraged. "What do you have in mind?"

"Here's what I would like her to do," Alexis explained. "We are going to start her off with simpler tasks like greeting and engaging with families when they come and build her up to where she's able to interview the nonoffending caregiver about what happened. That will be the end goal. To help her get there, I have some readings for her on models of working with families where sexual abuse has taken place, some readings on how to do family assessments, and a book on motivational interviewing. For assignments, I want to start off by having her create a list of therapists that do trauma-focused work with children. Later I want us to develop a nonoffending caregiver support group.

So I want her to research those. I think between completing assignments and working with families, she'll learn a lot. How does that sound?"

"I think that sounds like a great plan," Lorena answered. "But remember that she's new to this and she'll have a learning curve. Just keep me posted on how it's going and let me know if I can help."

### THE FIRST DAY OF PLACEMENT (AUGUST 24)

On the first day of the placement, Kim knocked lightly on Lorena's office door and said, "Hi, I'm here."

When she looked up, Lorena was surprised by Kim's appearance. Kim was dressed in flip-flops, pants whose cuffs were dragging on the ground, and a tight-fitting shirt that showed what Lorena considered a large amount of cleavage. *I want to be sensitive to her size and any issues she has with clothing*, Lorena thought, *but I need to address this with her. I guess this is our first "teaching moment."*

"Hi, Kim. It's nice to see you again. I'm looking forward to the upcoming year. I asked you to stop by so we could check in." Lorena tried to be gentle in how she presented her concern. "But before we do that, I want to talk about how you're dressed today."

She paused to see whether Kim would respond. But when she didn't, Lorena continued. "Because our kids have been sexualized way too early in their lives, we dress conservatively and professionally and do not wear any revealing clothing such as short dresses, low-cut tops, etc. We also interact a lot with other professionals like law enforcement and county child protection, and we should present a professional image to them and our families. We expect and need for you to wear professional attire. If you look at how others dress while in the office—me, for example—you'll see what I mean by professional. Do you have any questions about what we need from you in terms of dress?"

"No," Kim responded without expression, "I understand. I'll follow the dress code. There won't be any more concerns."

Lorena asked Kim a few questions about her summer and gave her an update on recent events at Ozark Alliance before walking her down to Alexis's office. *She didn't seem at all embarrassed or uncomfortable about my confronting her about inappropriate dress*, Lorena thought as she returned to her own office. *How odd.*

Lorena could tell from the look on Alexis's face that something was bothering her.

"I just don't understand her, Lorena," Alexis began. "I ask Kim to do something. She says she will, and then she doesn't."

"Tell me more about what you mean, Alexis," Lorena encouraged.

"Well, on her first day I gave her the list of assignments we discussed. She said that she was fine with them. Last Wednesday I asked her to greet a family that was coming in for an interview and gave her explicit instructions on what to do. I asked if she had any questions, and she said, 'No.' I stood in the hall and watched as she sheepishly greeted them at the door and offered them a place to sit in the waiting room. Then she just went into the student's office and started doing something on the computer. I couldn't believe it. I waited a moment to see if she was going to come out. When she didn't, I took care of the family myself."

"Did you talk to her about not staying with the family?" Lorena asked.

"Not then," Alexis explained. "I just jumped in to help the family. I didn't want them left alone. I asked her about it later, and she said she misunderstood me. But I don't know how that's possible. Then she called in sick on Thursday. On Friday, I asked her about the assignments I gave her. All she said was 'I'll get started on them.' "

"Maybe Kim was just overwhelmed by being here five days for block week. It can be intense here," Lorena cautioned. "How did she do this week?"

"Let's see," Alexis responded. "I emailed her over the weekend to tell her we had a family coming in on Monday. She called in sick Monday."

"That's not a good sign," Lorena interjected.

"On Wednesday, she was to work on her assignments, but she had nothing to show me. I have found her on Facebook and her cell phone a couple of times. I don't know if that had anything to do with it or not."

"Her behavior's hard to understand," Lorena agreed. "When I give instructions, I often find that it helps to have someone repeat back what I have said. You might want to try that with her," Lorena suggested. "Let's see how it goes next week, and if it doesn't get better, I'll intervene."

"Okay," Alexis stated. "I'll give it a shot and let you know what happens."

## SUPERVISION WITH LORENA AND ALEXIS (SEPTEMBER 11)

"How are things going with Kim?" Lorena asked Alexis at their next supervision meeting.

"Nothing's changed, really," Alexis reported. "I asked Kim to greet a family that came in on Monday. She said she knew what to do but acted essentially the way she did with the first family. I asked her on Wednesday to show me what she had completed on her assignments, and she said that she would, but nothing ever materialized.

"Do I need to talk with her?" Lorena asked.

"Yes, please!" Alexis responded, frustration evident in her voice. "I don't know how you supervised students all of these years!" Alexis exclaimed. "I'm not sure I have the patience for it."

"Well, this is an unusual case," Lorena assured her. "I'll talk to her on Monday."

## LORENA'S MEETING WITH KIM (SEPTEMBER 14)

"Hi, Kim," Lorena began tentatively. She wasn't quite sure how to approach Kim. In all her years of supervising students, she had not encountered this kind of student problem before. "I wanted to meet with you to talk about how things are going. I've spoken to Alexis, and she expressed some concerns about your performance, Kim. Let's start by talking about your approach to engaging with our families as they come in. I know from Alexis that you have worked with two families that came in for interviews."

"Okay," Kim agreed.

"When they come in and you are out in the waiting area talking with the child," Lorena asked, "do you understand what your role is out there?"

"No, not really."

"Remember, part of our responsibility is to ensure that whatever the kids and families are talking about, it's not about the abuse that's under investigation. So they need supervision the whole time they're together. And remember that the kids are often pretty nervous about coming here, so you could sit at the table with some coloring pages and color with the child. You could ask about where they go to school, what their favorite things are. It doesn't matter as long as you are creating a safe space for them and they aren't talking about the alleged abuse."

"Okay," Kim said.

"Let's practice. Let's say I am a five-year-old who has come in with his mother, the nonoffending caregiver. You greet me at the door. Tell me what you would say."

"Um," Kim hesitated, "I'm not sure."

"That's why we're practicing," Lorena encouraged. "Go ahead and try to respond."

Slowly, Kim began, "Hi. How are you today?"

"Good." After a lengthy pause, "What next?" Lorena prompted.

"I don't know," Kim answered. "I could ask him if he wants to color."

"That's a possibility," Lorena said. "Let's do this. I'll model it for you, and then we'll have you practice it."

They continued the role play for another ten minutes, with Lorena modeling responses and then having Kim try them.

Lorena had learned to keep detailed notes on her supervision meetings during her days as a clinician. As part of the summary of her meeting with Kim, she wrote, "Kim has challenges using even basic active listening skills or following social etiquette." As Lorena wrote, she thought, *Considering Alexis's limited patience for poor performance, I hope I didn't make a big mistake by putting them together.*

### SUPERVISION WITH LORENA AND ALEXIS (SEPTEMBER 18)

Lorena was not looking forward to discussing Kim's performance during the weekly supervision with Alexis. She knew from her informal conversations with Alexis that things were not improving. She wasn't sure what advice to give Alexis.

"Well"—Lorena paused—"how are things going with Kim?" Lorena thought Alexis looked agitated as she sat down across from Lorena's desk.

"Nothing's changed," Alexis said in an exasperated tone.

"She does not seem to be able to interact with clients," Lorena commiserated, "not even in the simplest of ways. Even when I modeled responses for her during our role play, she struggled."

"Yes," Alexis agreed. "I don't understand it. It's almost like she's afraid of them. And with her assignments!" Alexis covered her eyes with her hand, tilted her head back, and took a deep breath. "She says she will do them, but then she just doesn't. I'm concerned that she isn't going to learn anything while she's here. I'm afraid this is a mean thing to say, but there does not appear to be much depth there. I don't know if we have anything to work with."

Lorena moved intuitively to her strengths-based perspective. "Well, she has a bachelor's degree, and she got accepted into an MSW program, so there must be something there."

Alexis shrugged her shoulders. "I know I can be pretty intolerant of incompetence, and I feel bad that my frustration with her is showing, but I don't even think she notices. She asked me the other day if she could use her field hours to attend a training in Cape Girardeau. It almost feels like she doesn't want to be here. She's missed three days already. And when she's here, I still find her on her cell phone and Facebook even though I asked her not to do that. I don't think I can last a whole year with her."

"Okay, well, I'll call the field liaison to set up a meeting regarding our expectations and see if that helps any," Lorena suggested.

"Okay," Alexis said hesitantly, "please do that."

### THE MEETING WITH THE FIELD LIAISON (SEPTEMBER 23)

When field liaison Robert Cramer arrived, Lorena had Kim provide him a tour of the building. After the tour, Lorena, Alexis, Robert, and Kim sat in a conference room.

"I'm impressed with the services offered here," Robert began. "I've been hearing a lot of good things about the CAC model. Alexis, Lorena, thank you for taking on an intern this year. This seems like a great placement site, and the school appreciates your contribution." Then, turning to Kim, he said, "We're having this meeting earlier than I normally schedule them, but I was asked to come out to help clarify performance expectations and tasks. Who would like to start?"

After a moment, Alexis began. "There seems to be a disconnect between our understanding of what's required for placement and Kim's. We've asked Kim to do a number of things for her learning and professional growth, as well as to help the CAC, and Kim does not seem to understand the importance of completing these tasks."

"I'm not sure how to say this, Kim," Alexis turned toward Kim, "but are you sure that this is the right place for you?"

Kim did not answer.

"It helps to look at these things in terms of the learning contract," Robert suggested. "It should be our guiding document when it comes to evaluation of performance. Do you have a copy of it I can see?"

"Yes," Alexis stated. "I have it here and can show you the things I'm talking about." Alexis offered a copy of the learning contract and walked the group through Kim's tasks.

"Kim," Robert said, turning to her, "do you agree with the tasks on your contract?"

"Yes," Kim replied.

"Do you understand what we're saying?" Lorena interjected. She was not sure whether Kim understood the gravity of the discussion. "We want to keep you here, but it's contingent on you meeting the requirements outlined in your contract."

"Yes, I understand," Kim said, nodding, "and I can do the things you are asking."

"Is there anything that the school or I or your supervisors here can do to help you?" Robert asked.

"No," Kim replied. "I can do the things everyone is asking me to do."

"There is something else that is bothering me," Alexis added after a brief pause. "Kim, I don't want you to spend so much time here on Facebook or on your cell phone. I think these are distracting you from your work."

Kim did not respond.

"So," Robert said, "let me see if I can sum up what's been said so far." He summarized Alexis's and Lorena's concerns and Kim's responses and then said, "Let's do an action plan. Here's what I suggest." Turning to Kim, he said, "You're going to complete all of the tasks and assignments on your learning contract. You will meet regularly with your supervisors to discuss your progress. You cannot bring your cell phone into the building. You cannot be on Facebook at the internship. Can we agree on this?"

"Yes," Kim replied.

"I think this is a very good plan," Lorena affirmed. "Follow through with this and things will go well."

"I'll keep doing my part," Alexis added. But Lorena thought she noticed uncertainty in Alexis's voice.

## AN UNANTICIPATED REQUEST (SEPTEMBER 28)

The following week Alexis sent an email to Lorena indicating that Kim wanted to meet with them to talk about spending some time in the WRC. Lorena agreed and anticipated the knock on her door a few minutes later.

"Come on in," Lorena said when she heard the knock.

After they sat down, Kim looked at Alexis, who said, "Go ahead, Kim."

Kim turned to Lorena and said, "I think I'd like to go next door and work with the program director on a grant for WRC. As you know, I'm a trained advocate, and I want to learn more about how it works."

Lorena hesitated and then said, "I'm concerned about you switching gears at this point. We have an action plan that we just made with the help of your liaison, and I think we need to follow it."

Lorena looked at Alexis and back at Kim and then said, "Is there something we can do to help you with it?"

Kim was quiet for a moment and then said, "No. I will just continue to work on the things you have given me to do. Thank you for meeting with me."

Kim turned to Alexis and said, "Thank you, Alexis." As Kim stood up and left Lorena's office, Alexis rolled her eyes at Lorena.

## LORENA'S MEETING WITH ALEXIS (SEPTEMBER 30)

"I don't know why I'm surprised that she called in sick today," Alexis said, sticking her head in Lorena's office early Wednesday morning.

"We have to think through this a bit," Lorena said, taking a deep breath. "We just committed to Kim and the liaison that we would follow the action plan."

"I know we did, Lorena," Alexis stated almost pleadingly, "but I don't know what I can do with her."

"I have to admit that I feel guilty about this. I thought it was going to be a great thing for you to have a student," Lorena offered apologetically, "and usually it is."

"Well, it hasn't been," Alexis stated emphatically. "She's the most stressful part of my job. Around here, that's saying a lot. But I have a meeting with a guardian ad litem now, so can we talk about this more during tomorrow's supervision?"

"Of course," Lorena answered. "Let's do that. We'll figure it out then."

After Alexis left her office, Lorena wondered, almost aloud, *What do I do now? We just agreed to an action plan with Kim and the school, and I think we need to honor that agreement. But are we just setting her up for failure? And what about Alexis? Is it fair to ask her to continue working with Kim? She's at her wit's end, and I can't afford to antagonize her over this.*

# 7

# HANDLING ADVERSITY

*Meredith C. F. Powers and Terry A. Wolfer*

Wondering what to expect, field liaison Sarah Jennings opened an email from Vanessa Glen, one of her field students:

> Hi, I want to know if you are free to meet? I want to discuss the possibility of changing field placements. I can help with the process of finding another one if necessary. I do not mind calling around myself. I am still advocating for myself and trying to gain the best experience for the amount of money I am spending on graduate school. I hope you have a great day. Hope to hear from you soon.

---

This decision case was prepared solely to provide material for class discussion and not to suggest either effective or ineffective handling of the situation depicted. While based on field research regarding an actual situation, names and certain facts may have been disguised to protect confidentiality. The authors wish to thank the case reporter for cooperation in making this account available for the benefit of social work students and practitioners.

*What?* Sarah reacted. *I thought we resolved her issues at our meeting a couple weeks ago. Now what should I do?*

## CHATHAM COUNTY, NORTH CAROLINA

Chatham County was situated in the middle of the state. It had a population of approximately 63,500, disaggregated as 71 percent white, 13 percent African American, 12 percent Hispanic/Latino, 2 percent Asian, and 2 percent who self-reported as "other." School-age children and youth made up 22 percent of the population. The average income was approximately $46,500; however, 10.3 percent had incomes below the poverty line and resided in pockets of extreme poverty.

In 2011, school administrators in Chatham County developed the Yellow Zone Project (YZP) to streamline identification of and ensure interventions for students who had chronic disciplinary problems (i.e., students at risk for behavioral health problems, students with four or more disciplinary referrals, students with current or past trauma experience including separation from military parents, students found possessing an unauthorized item at school, and/or students with poor attendance). The primary interventions of the YZP included increasing social work services, expanding student assistance teams, and offering targeted mentoring services.

The increased need for professional intervention with children in the YZP highlighted the absence of social workers in Chatham County schools. Thus, William Johnson, the grants director for the Chatham County School District, initiated a partnership between the district and the University of North Carolina (UNC). Together, the district and the Field Education Office in the School of Social Work (SSW) developed a special internship project that provided foundation-year MSW field placements in six Chatham County schools. It was structured so that each MSW student was placed at a separate school in the district, where they would work alongside the school principal, teachers, and counselors. Because district schools had no MSWs on staff to serve as field instructors, the students had on-site preceptors who oversaw their daily tasks, and Laurel Edwards, an off-site MSW social worker and School of Social Work (SSW) doctoral student, provided social work supervision to the students in a group format once every two weeks. In addition, Sarah Jennings served as the field liaison for the students, linking the SSW and the field setting.

Pittsboro Elementary School was one of the Chatham County schools that had an MSW field intern. The population at this school included students who lived in poor, rural areas, some in mobile homes without proper sanitation. Of approximately five hundred children enrolled at Pittsboro Elementary School, about 40 percent received free/reduced-price lunches.

During the first year of the project, MSW student Jenny Smith was assigned to Pittsboro Elementary School. On one occasion, early in her placement, Jenny encountered a child who came to school with a flea infestation resulting from an unsanitary home environment. She was very compassionate toward the child and tried hard not to make the family feel like something was wrong with them. She readily involved herself in the school, engaging with both children and school staff, and she was quick to initiate relationships and activities. Everyone at Pittsboro Elementary School raved about her, and staff were eager to have another MSW student in the second year of the project.

## KAREN JORDAN, PRECEPTOR

Karen Jordan was a school counselor with a bubbly disposition who had grown up in North Carolina and had worked at Pittsboro Elementary School for four years. She was white, was in her late twenties, had brown hair, and dressed like a traditional schoolteacher. She served as both the on-site preceptor for the MSW student at Pittsboro Elementary School and the supervisor for a school counseling student who was also interning there one day a week. She had a space in her office where the social work and counseling students could work.

## DR. SARAH JENNINGS, FIELD LIAISON

Dr. Sarah Jennings was white, was in her late thirties, wore glasses, and had brown, shoulder-length hair. She had her MSW and PhD from the UNC's SSW. Her twelve years of practice experience in the mental health sector included five years in public mental health practice and seven years in private mental health practice. For ten years during this period, she served as an MSW field instructor. She then left her practice in mental health and spent the past five years working at UNC as a full-time clinical professor, where her responsibilities included serving as a field liaison.

As a field liaison, Sarah coordinated field placements with the field instructors and preceptors, serving as the SSW's representative to ensure that students were getting the learning experiences required by the curriculum. Even though the SSW required field liaisons to visit field sites only once per semester, usually at midsemester, she valued getting to know all of her assigned students individually. She often told her colleagues that she saw her liaison role as "monitoring the pedagogical integrity of the placement." In that role, she explained, "I want to do things that empower the students and support their growth and not do things that feel punitive or pejorative." She enjoyed reaching out to students not only to make sure the placements met their learning needs but also to ensure these were comfortable settings for them. She prided herself on being very responsive to the students with whom she worked.

In 2012–2013, Sarah was field liaison for the six MSW students placed at six Chatham County schools, including a student at Pittsboro Elementary School. However, early in the semester the Field Education Office moved one of the students to a different field site because she was a second-year student and needed more advanced-practice opportunities than the YZP placement offered. This project with the Chatham County School District was intended only for foundation students, and the office quickly corrected the placement oversight.

### LAUREL EDWARDS, FIELD INSTRUCTOR

Laurel Edwards, a white woman in her midforties, had extensive practice experience. Most recently, she had worked for seven years at a local agency that served the homeless populations in North Carolina. While there, she served as a field instructor for MSW interns. At this same time, she was a doctoral student at UNC, where she also worked part-time as a research assistant.

From the outset of the YZP, Laurel was the off-site field instructor for the MSW students placed with the Chatham County School District. For these field students, she offered a group supervision model that provided them the opportunity to talk about school social work issues and individual cases. The group met every two weeks, beginning the first week of September. She was quite intentional about what she addressed in group supervision, but she would also meet with students for one-on-one supervision, as needed.

Sarah and Laurel developed a strong relationship during the first year of the YZP. From what Sarah could tell, Laurel was an excellent off-site field instructor, being very engaged with students and attentive and responsive to their learning needs. If Laurel was busy when students contacted her about something, she usually responded within the hour and always within twenty-four hours. In a few situations that required Sarah's intervention, Laurel worked well with Sarah and the students. Because they had a trusting relationship, Sarah felt comfortable talking with Laurel about student issues and relying on her to maintain confidentiality and help resolve problems. Sarah also considered Laurel a good mediator because she was able to maintain neutrality during field liaison meetings.

## STARTING THE SECOND YEAR OF THE YELLOW ZONE PROJECT

*I'm excited to serve as a field liaison for the Chatham County schools again this year,* Sarah thought, *especially because it's such a great project. The first year was a fantastic success; everyone—administrators, teachers, and students—loved having the MSW students working there. And the MSW students said they really learned a lot and were able to integrate fully their class learning into the field site. The administrators also indicated that the MSW students had a positive impact on the community and the school, as they were able to work with elementary students and families to get them needed resources.* She was especially excited to be working alongside Laurel as the field instructor for the project again this year. It was early September, and she had already started corresponding with the students, preceptors, and field instructors via email to schedule the field liaison meetings for October.

Although Sarah had not yet met Vanessa Glen, the field office supplied some background and contact information. Vanessa, a first-year MSW student, was placed at Pittsboro Elementary School for her internship, with Karen Jordan as her preceptor. She had no previous social work experience. Her student file indicated that she had a work-study assignment on campus one day each week in addition to her full-time load as an MSW student and her field practicum.

Sarah emailed Vanessa the first week of September, about two weeks after the field placement began. Sarah used this email was to check in and to finalize a date for the field liaison visit, which was set for October 23. In reply, Vanessa submitted her learning contract and noted that she liked the placement.

## VANESSA AND AMY REQUEST A MEETING

On October 14, one week before the scheduled liaison meeting, Sarah received an email from Vanessa:

> Hi, I hope your weekend went well. Amy Foster [another student in a Chatham school placement] and I wanted to know if you were free October 21 or 22 to meet. We wanted to speak with you before our scheduled field liaison meetings at the schools. We hope to hear from you soon.

*Hmmm, I wonder what that's about. Maybe they want to tell me something to prepare me for the liaison meetings*, Sarah mused, *and share what some of their concerns might be.*

The next day Sarah replied and suggested meeting on October 21 after their afternoon classes.

"That day is perfect for us," Vanessa emailed promptly. "We will see you then. Thanks!"

*I wonder what's going on*, Sarah thought. *No clue in the email.*

## THE MEETING WITH VANESSA AND AMY

At the scheduled time, Vanessa and Amy came to Sarah's faculty office. They sat down in chairs across from Sarah's desk. Vanessa, an African

American, was in her early twenties and slightly overweight, with straightened hair. She wore no makeup and was dressed professionally, like a schoolteacher. Amy was white and also in her early twenties. She appeared a bit shy and was dressed professionally.

Skipping the small talk, Vanessa looked at Sarah and said, "I have had no opportunity to do anything at the placement, and I want to be at a placement where there is an on-site social work field instructor, and I don't want to be somewhere where I don't feel that I'm getting the most for my money. Amy feels the same way I do."

Amy didn't comment but nodded along.

"Well," Sarah began, "have you talked to Laurel about this?"

"No. Well," Vanessa continued, "we really haven't had a chance in our supervision meetings to talk about this. We been talking about content, and we talked some about our placements. But I know I can switch placements because the other student in our supervision group this semester already switched out of her placement."

"Well"—Sarah paused, surprised—"that was a second-year student placed there by mistake. But I know that the student last year had all different kinds of opportunities at Pittsboro Elementary School. Are people at your placement coming to you with opportunities?"

"No, not really," Vanessa responded in a deadpan manner. "I don't really feel like I have an opportunity to do much. I have to say something: people really aren't giving me anything to do at the placement."

Sarah was not sure how to interpret Vanessa's affect. But she wanted to accept what Vanessa was saying and sought to take her concern seriously.

"Okay, let's go ahead with our scheduled liaison visit with your preceptor, Karen, and your field instructor, Laurel. It's set for October 23, which is just two days away. Perhaps at that meeting we can figure things out with your preceptor. And perhaps I can role model for you how you can attend to that conflict with your preceptor and others at your placement. I can teach you how to ask for what you want and what you need."

When Vanessa didn't respond, Sarah turned to Amy to get her perspective.

"So, Amy, how are you doing at your school? Are you getting what you need?"

"Well, it was slow at first," Amy responded, "but now I'm really getting into it. I did feel like Vanessa at the beginning, but I don't really feel that way anymore."

*Hmmm*, Sarah thought, *this seems like a different story. I wonder if there is a little information contagion going on here, since Vanessa brought up the other student who was discontented and changed placements. I think I had better separate these two and check in with them both individually.*

"Can I meet with each of you individually to talk about your issues," Sarah asked, "because I don't want to get too much into the ethics of sharing too much with each other?"

Amy and Vanessa decided Amy could go first because it wouldn't take her as long. Vanessa waited in the lobby outside Sarah's office while Sarah and Amy chatted.

"So, Amy, tell me what's going on," Sarah requested.

"I really just came to support Vanessa," Amy said, almost apologetically. "I don't have a problem. Again, like I said earlier, in the beginning it was a slow start, but now I'm fine. Things are working out well with my preceptor. But I think I would benefit from having a social worker supervise me on-site. Sometimes it's hard for me, but I think it's getting easier, and I have been able to process it in the group supervision sessions with Laurel."

Sarah thanked Amy and excused her. Then she called Vanessa back into her office.

"So, Vanessa, let's see what we can do to help you with your concerns," Sarah began.

"Well, like I said, I'm not getting the opportunity to do much," Vanessa repeated. "And I'm not going to be paying for education as a service and be in a placement that I am not satisfied with. I want to have a caseload. I want to do client work."

"Well, Vanessa," Sarah replied evenly, "you're not really prepared to do that yet. You're not an advanced-year student." *I could see an advanced-year student making that claim*, Sarah thought, *but that's not valid for a foundation-year student*. "You see, foundation-year students may not yet have the knowledge and skills to work directly with clients one-on-one. In fact, foundation-year students technically shouldn't even have interactions alone with clients the first semester because they need to learn and observe things and shadow a preceptor or supervisor and be able to process them first. This is part of the reason why foundation-year students are encouraged to do process recordings and have discussions with their field instructors. In addition, it is important to understand that the concept of client does not necessarily mean a therapy client. A client could be an individual, family, or group. So if a student is working in a school, client contact may look a little different than when they have a caseload of individual clients. So your work in the school may look a little different than what you may have expected, but it will give you client contact and opportunities to observe Karen working with those various types of clients. We can also discuss this at the liaison meeting and see how Karen could perhaps offer you more opportunities, like shadowing her during sessions with clients."

"Well, there is not really enough individual supervision from Karen. And she seems busy with the counseling student she supervises," Vanessa stated. "Also, I want to take the lead on a project."

"Well, we actually have placements where there are three students at the same placement, and they have to learn how to handle that. Perhaps you could see this as an opportunity for interprofessional collaboration. Maybe you could partner with the counseling student on a project," Sarah suggested, trying to find a positive angle to use as a starting point. "I imagine there would be an opportunity for you to practice some leadership skills at your placement. All these are things we should discuss at our liaison meeting with your preceptor. *Maybe*, Sarah thought to herself, *I could help translate for her and help advocate for some of the things she wants because she seems to simply not have enough opportunities and she wants more opportunities to lead.*

"I'm going to help you advocate for more opportunities. Again, I know the student before you had a lot of opportunities to engage in activities." *So I don't think it's a problem with the placement itself*, Sarah mused. *Maybe Karen is comparing Vanessa to the counseling student or the MSW student from the previous year. That may be a lot of pressure for her, but that's life, and you have to learn how to deal with it. I just need to figure out how to put in the extra supports she needs because I think she really does have the capacity to succeed.*

"Well, I'm actually a little nervous about the upcoming liaison meeting," Vanessa noted. "It feels overwhelming, us talking as a whole group about these problems."

"Okay, I can understand that," Sarah said reassuringly, "but you need to remember that we are all there just to help you get a good learning experience. It is also important for me, as your liaison, to know what you want to accomplish out of the meeting. I think the placement has great potential for being a good field placement for you. So let's have the liaison meeting as scheduled and talk about it as a group and see if they can give you what you need. It is also important for me to understand everybody's perspective, so I am going to have to check in with your field instructor and preceptor at our liaison meeting. But I am looking forward to our meeting with them to help advocate for you."

*It's hard*, Sarah thought, *but this is the great thing about the role of field liaison. You listen to the student, but you also have a responsibility to listen to the field instructor about what's going on. You're supposed to be the independent intermediary to decide about what's going on and what the next steps should be to address the entire situation.*

"So shall we plan to keep our scheduled liaison meeting?" Sarah asked.

"I guess so," Vanessa said with a shrug as she stood to leave. "Thanks for talking."

*Wow*, Sarah thought after Vanessa left her office, *she is so hard to read. I hope she feels that she is supported and that we can work these issues out at the meeting. She seems to take her education very seriously and really wants to learn as a social work student so she can better help people. I like that she took initiative and advocated for herself by contacting me when she wasn't happy about something at her field site.*

Sarah decided to call Laurel to talk about what might be going on and to brainstorm ways to get Vanessa what she wanted from her field experience. "Based on what Vanessa told me," Sarah told Laurel, "the school is clueless that she is having any problems. Because I haven't heard from them, I'm thinking that they are satisfied with her performance and that they are fine with everything. But we really need to make sure it is the best educational experience for Vanessa."

"Interesting," Laurel responded. "Vanessa hasn't expressed anything to me about her concerns and we've had four supervision sessions so far. Also, the student who was placed there last year had such a good learning experience. She was at the same school, under the same preceptor, so that makes me think it's a good placement. But I'm not sure what's going on with Vanessa. Let's have the liaison meeting and see what we can do to adjust it."

## THE LIAISON MEETING FOR VANESSA

Sarah and Laurel drove together to Pittsboro Elementary School to meet Karen and Vanessa. They both saw this meeting as an opportunity to ensure Vanessa had a beneficial placement and to support their relationship.

They walked into the school and were directed to the library. Karen and Vanessa greeted them and introduced Jody Nichols, the principal, who wanted to join the meeting. *It doesn't seem like Karen and Vanessa are connecting with each other too well*, Sarah thought while observing their nonverbal cues, *or this could be more evidence of Vanessa's flat affect. Let's see how this meeting goes.* They all sat around a small table with child-sized chairs. It was not ideal, but they were all relatively comfortable. Sarah asked questions regarding opportunities available at the placement. Without technically summarizing the concerns Vanessa had brought to her attention at their meeting two days before, she elicited discussion around these points to offer Vanessa an opportunity to voice her concerns. Karen seemed surprised that Vanessa didn't feel she was getting as much attention as the counseling student Karen supervised, and she assured Sarah that that counseling student would be there only until her practicum was completed at the end of the fall semester. But Karen also liked the idea of interdisciplinary collaboration and thought that there would be opportunities for Vanessa and the counseling student to do projects together even though the learning aims of that program were different from the ones for the social work program in terms of competency development. Nevertheless, Karen was pleased that Vanessa wanted to take a lead in something. Karen also noted a couple of times how great the previous MSW student was and the variety of things she had done the year before.

Sarah winced. *Let's not spend time in this meeting on talking about what took place last year or making comparisons with the previous student. I prefer to focus on helping this student succeed.* So Sarah said, "How about we look at the learning contract and see what learning objectives can be met and what areas we may need to change. Let's talk about things Vanessa could do that would be a good marriage with the curriculum, including class assignments, such as the psychosocial assessment and a group proposal project."

So as a group they discussed the details of those opportunities and how Vanessa could take the lead on a project. Together, they came up with a plan for Vanessa to lead a presentation toward the end of the semester to the Hispanic/Latino parent group at the school. In it, she would set out ways for them to become more knowledgeable about services and ways they could access things in the school district.

At the end of this discussion, Sarah gently brought attention to Vanessa's flat affect, saying "Vanessa, sometimes it is a little hard to read your nonverbal cues. And I wonder if working on that could help with better communication at your field placement?"

"It would be nice," Karen confirmed, "if kids at school could look at you and see positive affirmation, on some level, some sort of indication."

"Yes," Vanessa said and cracked a bit of a smile. Then Vanessa asked Sarah, "Can you look at the presentation before I give it?"

"Sure," Sarah agreed. "Let's check in closer to the time you give it. I would be happy to give you feedback."

## THE FINAL EMAIL DILEMMA

Two weeks after the field liaison meeting, Sarah received the following email from Laurel:

> Hi, Sarah. I just spoke to Karen, who informed me that two days prior to the field liaison meeting we just had with Vanessa and Karen, she and Principal Nichols had confronted Vanessa about her low initiative, her lack of follow-through when she's asked to do something menial, and her writing skill level. Evidently they talked to her about their concerns a few days before the liaison meeting we had with them, and they are keeping an eye on how she takes their direction. I emailed Vanessa and set a meeting with her tomorrow to talk to her about the importance of teamwork, and I will also talk to her about her writing and see if she needs extra support. It was a very good talk

> with Karen. She did say that she thinks the student has potential. I think so, too. Do you have any words of advice? Or is there anything else you'd like to see me do?

Sarah didn't respond to Laurel's email immediately because she noticed an email from Vanessa waiting in her inbox. *Let me see what Vanessa wrote first*, Sarah thought, as she opened Vanessa's email:

> Hi, I want to know if you are free to meet? I want to discuss the possibility of changing field placements. I can help with the process of finding another one if necessary. I do not mind calling around myself. I am still advocating for myself and trying to gain the best experience for the amount of money I am spending on graduate school. I hope you have a great day. Hope to hear from you soon.

*What?* Sarah reacted. *I thought we resolved her issues at our meeting a couple weeks ago. Now what should I do?*

# 8

## WHO TO FIRE?

*Sara J. English and Terry A. Wolfer*

"Not every person is right for every placement," said the field instructor Corporal Beth Poole with a shrug.

"But what about the other students?" Dr. Ellen Demitri asked. She served as the program's field liaison and could hardly believe what Cpl. Poole was saying during their debriefing following the student orientation. "What does it say to them if we fire their classmate before the placement even begins? How can we create a positive learning environment if we don't allow our students to learn?"

Cpl. Poole looked at Dr. Demitri and shrugged. "Well, people get fired all the time. But it's your program," she sighed. "I think we should have a meeting, just the three of us."

---

This decision case was prepared solely to provide material for class discussion and not to suggest either effective or ineffective handling of the situation depicted. While based on field research regarding an actual situation, names and certain facts may have been disguised to protect confidentiality. The authors wish to thank the case reporter for cooperation in making this account available for the benefit of social work students and practitioners.

After the conversation, as Dr. Demitri walked down the hallway, she reflected about how difficult the placement selection process had been. *I'm just not sure what is right*, she pondered. *One day Beth is for Lisa; the next day she isn't. Maybe she's right. Then, again, shouldn't we be responsible for educating students on how their professional conduct impacts practice and how they can improve?*

## FAIRFAX COUNTY POLICE DEPARTMENT

The mission of the Fairfax County Police Department (FCPD), located in northern Virginia, was to prevent and fight crime. Through its highly engaged community outreach, it maintained a reputation as one of the safest major jurisdictions in the United States. Chief of Police Bill Walpole was the popular leader of the FCPD. He had led the department for almost twenty years and was generally well liked. During his tenure, both Chief Walpole and the FCPD had been recognized for excellence by community and national organizations. Chief Walpole believed the success of the FCPD could be attributed to the rapport that existed between the community and the department, which he worked hard to maintain.

## SCHOOL RESOURCE OFFICER PROGRAM

The School Resource Officer (SRO) Program was a collaborative effort that involved the FCPD, educators, students, parents, and the community and that placed SROs in middle and high schools throughout the Fairfax County School District. It included trained law enforcement personnel who utilized a collaborative "Triple Concept," with each SRO serving three functions within the school: law-related educator, counselor, and mentor. Each SRO was assigned to one school, and that school became the officer's appointment, with the officer serving as a role model and liaison between the school-based community and the FCPD.

## CORPORAL BETH POOLE

Cpl. Beth Poole, a white woman of Spanish descent in her midthirties, had completed her MSW degree at George Mason University. Following her graduation, she joined the FCPD and dedicated her life to what she described as "making a difference." She had been on the force for several years and believed her social work training helped her succeed in the highly charged emotional situations that often occurred in law enforcement. Her office was located at a substation close to the university campus. Over time, she had advanced and had been promoted to field instructor of the SRO Program for the district.

## SCHOOL OF SOCIAL WORK AND OFFICE OF FIELD EDUCATION

George Mason University was established in Fairfax County in 1956 as a branch of the University of Virginia. It became an independent public research university in 1972. Its SSW set as its goal providing students with the "essential knowledge, skills, and values to practice effectively, ethically, and collaboratively to promote social well-being and social justice for vulnerable populations," and its MSW program had almost six hundred students. The mission of the MSW program was to prepare graduates as advanced practitioners who served diverse communities, and field education was an essential part of every MSW student's professional training.

The SSW's Office of Field Education collaborated with more than five hundred social work professionals and four hundred social service organizations to provide field education for BSW and MSW students at the university. All two-year MSW students had to complete two different field placements, each more than five hundred hours long: a generalist field placement in their first year and a specialization field placement in their second year. Students who entered the MSW program with a BSW degree and met the admission criteria were admitted to the advanced-standing program, where they could substitute their BSW field placement experience for the foundation-year placement, completing the MSW program in twelve months.

Dr. Betty Smith, director of field education, believed that the success of the program depended on strong, positive relationships between the SSW and the community organizations that volunteered to provide field education placements for students. In keeping with the mission of the Office of Field Education, MSW students were seen as representatives of the SSW. They were expected to abide by the National

Association of Social Workers' Code of Ethics, exhibiting professional behavior at all times.

The Office of Field Education provided oversight for field students via field liaisons (faculty, staff, or doctoral students), appointed to maintain a direct link among the SSW, field students, and field instructors. Both field students and field instructors relied on these field liaisons to provide guidance regarding learning opportunities. In addition, field liaisons served as the point of contact for problems regarding the organization or student performance.

## FCPD FIELD PRACTICUM

The FCPD Field Practicum began in 2009 as a collaborative effort between the FCPD and the SSW. Chief Walpole was interested in developing a relationship between the FCPD and the university and believed the SRO Program would be enhanced by incorporating social work students. After contacting the SSW, Chief Walpole and Dr. Edgar Joss, a long-time professor of social work, developed the FCPD Field Practicum, which focused on at-risk sixth-grade students. The target group usually included twenty to thirty at-risk students. The two men believed that the practicum could help reduce school dropout rates, drug use, and other problematic behaviors. Dr. Joss also believed the practicum would benefit MSW students through the real-world experience it would provide, introducing them to the work environments of both the FCPD and the school system.

The MSW students who applied for the FCPD Field Practicum were rigorously vetted with multiple interviews, a law enforcement background check, a drug test, and a polygraph test. These requirements deterred some potential applicants, and negative results excluded a few others. Additionally, students selected for the practicum were required to attend a half-day workshop with the SROs before their placements began.

At the beginning of the FCPD Field Practicum, field students interviewed various school staff members, attended interdisciplinary meetings in schools, reviewed documentation, and identified potential at-risk students. Subsequently, field students had two primary responsibilities. First, they shadowed an SRO and participated in SRO-related activities, such as crisis intervention or drug searches. Second, they carried a caseload, working one-on-one with at-risk students.

In her role as field instructor, Cpl. Poole initially provided direct supervision for the MSW field students, with Dr. Joss serving as the field liaison for the SSW and providing her support. Although the practicum began with sixth-grade students at one school, it expanded over six years to include sixth-grade students at four schools across the district. As the program grew, Cpl. Poole was promoted from SRO to the role of FCPD field instructor and helped lead the FCPD Field Practicum. As Cpl. Poole told colleagues, "I enjoy the program. It lets me use my social work skills and helps MSW students connect with our kids."

The FCPD had always provided positive feedback for the practicum, and the field placement contract was renewed each year; yet feedback from the MSW students was not always positive. There had been complaints from students regarding the scheduling of group meetings between the students and Dr. Joss. To accommodate his schedule, he held these meetings at seven A.M. One student who lived more than an hour away labeled this "unreasonable" and "unfair." Also, several students noted that his lecture style did not create a seminar environment that would encourage discussion about social work practice and the dilemmas students faced in the practicum.

## DR. ELLEN DEMITRI

Dr. Ellen Demitri was a white, thirty-something assistant professor of social work at George Mason University. She had a strong interdisciplinary background and had worked with persons of diverse experience and expertise. She was an experienced grants administrator and evaluation consultant for youth programs and held an MSW and a PhD in public health. Her ability to work with multiple disciplines enabled her to focus on ways programs could be developed to meet the holistic needs of participants and help individuals build capacity. As a tenure track assistant professor, she was eager to develop evidence-based programs. She enjoyed bringing research to the real world and developed action-oriented programs, making measurable change in the lives of children and youth. She had successfully developed programs throughout her relatively new academic career, and her experience made her a good choice to lead community-based programs.

Dr. Demitri believed that evidence-based programming could bring about sustainable change for persons who were vulnerable or at risk, especially youth. The FCPD Field Practicum offered an opportunity for her to apply her skills as a program developer to an existing program, allowing her to evaluate the program and create new interventions that affected real, measurable change for at-risk sixth-grade students.

## IN THE BEGINNING

Following Dr. Joss's retirement, the dean of the SSW tapped Dr. Demitri to lead the FCPD Field Practicum. As she was in her second year as an assistant professor, her time was limited, but she assumed responsibility for the practicum as one of her assigned courses. It was important for her to generate scholarship from the practicum, and she believed that new interventions would make real change in the lives of young persons. Additionally, she hoped to create a learning environment for the MSW students that would encourage seminar discussion and group learning.

In her first year leading the practicum, Dr. Demitri made no major changes to the overall program; however, she moved the start time for group supervision later in the day. In her second year, she began to map out the use of what she termed "compassionate conversation techniques," which aimed to influence positive changes in behavior for at-risk sixth-grade students. In her third year, following the development of a more structured intervention, she applied for and won an internal university grant to support incorporating this innovation into the practicum. In her fourth year, she was ready to pilot the revamped practicum, which she renamed COMPASS. "The COMPASS Program will be a lot of work," she confided to her colleagues, "but it will be worth the time and the outcomes for the kids."

Through the COMPASS Program, MSW field students learned how to engage in compassionate conversations with at-risk sixth-grade students and collected data on the effects of this intervention. Dr. Demitri shared her optimism about the program with Dr. Smith: "I'm really excited about the potential for the new intervention. The FCPD program has really grown. Instead of doing the same thing over and over, the students will really be able to effect real change in the lives of the kids who are at risk. Although the social work students work in different schools, they meet together in seminar and for group supervision. They form their own field of practice, keeping track of case notes, troubleshooting, and sharing ideas and information. It is important that they are able to work together. This new intervention also allows them to develop collaboration skills and a mastery of how to engage with and connect with students. I am eager to see where it goes."

Each week the MSW students discussed concerns and worked together to develop intervention strategies, with Cpl. Poole serving as field instructor and Dr. Demitri as field liaison. Both Cpl. Poole and Dr. Demitri participated in the weekly field seminar and shared responsibility for students' learning. Dr. Demitri enjoyed a positive working relationship with Cpl. Poole. While working with the FCPD Practicum, the two women spoke regularly, both in the field seminar and via telephone.

## RECRUITING A NEW MSW COHORT FOR COMPASS

At the end of the spring semester, before MSW students were selected for the fall placement, Dr. Demitri met with Cpl. Poole to iron out the details of the new intervention. "The new goals have a lot of potential, and they're adding something significant," she began. "With improved skills, the MSW students can give the sixth-grade kids some tools to make better choices. They will be able to develop significant helping relationships with the MSW students and be provided another way to think about how to make better choices."

"If you say so," Cpl. Poole said. "I am not so sure that all this work will be worth it. Change is not always a good thing. Things have been going well so far. I mean, we have been getting really good reviews about the program as things are."

*Well, this is new*, Dr. Demitri thought. She was perplexed by Cpl. Poole's reaction. *She has not voiced any concerns before. We've talked about the compassionate conversation aspect many times. Is Cpl. Poole still committed to the changes in the program?*

"I know it's hard to make changes," Dr. Demitri responded, "but these are things that can make a difference in the lives of the kids and the MSW students. I want our students to learn and understand the importance of what they're doing. I want them to get credit for all the hard work they'll be doing. I want them to be motivated by the changes that are possible and to believe that the things they do and the way they do them are meaningful."

"Maybe so," Cpl. Poole acknowledged half-heartedly.

"How can we expect them to be motivated if we aren't?" Dr. Demitri asked.

"I've worked really hard to establish a good relationship with her," Dr. Demitri confided to several colleagues later that week. "Up until now, I always thought she could say anything to me . . . and I thought I could say anything to her. I mean, we've become friends, as well as colleagues. I just want to be able to push this program a little bit. I want to implement something that's evidence-based and I want to be able to evaluate what we're doing."

By June, several MSW students had applied to the COMPASS Program for the fall semester, but none had completed the application process. Two students who applied were rejected due to a negative background check, and another student had a negative polygraph result.

By mid-June, Dr. Demitri became concerned because most of the MSW placements for the COMPASS Program remained unfilled. *The scheduled training for COMPASS is coming up*, she fretted. *I'm concerned we won't have enough students to fill the positions and may not be able to go forward.*

Dr. Demitri's worries were confirmed when Dr. Smith called. "Is there something going on with Cpl. Poole?" Dr. Smith asked. "Three students have refused to continue with the application process after a phone interview with Cpl. Poole. It's becoming very hard to fill these placements."

"I am not aware of anything going on with Cpl. Poole," Dr. Demitri replied.

"Well," Dr. Smith continued, "we've already sent some additional students for an interview, and I spoke to her personally about students reporting it was not a good fit. Look, I wanted to make you aware of what's going on. The students are saying that Cpl. Poole isn't very friendly, and students don't want to take a placement if they have a mentor with that disposition."

"We've never had a problem finding placements for this program before," Dr. Demitri responded. "Is there some way I can help? I suppose I could be more involved in the vetting process, but Cpl. Poole has always taken care of the interviews."

"Well, she isn't being very successful with her interviewing right now," Dr. Smith said.

Dr. Demitri paused for a moment and then replied, "You know, now that you mention it, Cpl. Poole has seemed a little disengaged compared to years past. Maybe there is something going on. I am a little hesitant, though, to get involved and disrupt how things have always been done. I don't want to upset the good working relationship I have with Cpl. Poole."

"Well, I just wanted to let you know about the problem. I think some of the difficulty we are experiencing in filling this placement may be because Cpl. Poole is coming off as disinterested," Dr. Smith continued. "Do you think you might speak with her about this?"

"Sure," Dr. Demitri offered. "I'll call her and see if she's concerned about anything about the program. We really need to have a certain number of students in order to move forward. I'll be sure to ask her if there's any way I can be more helpful."

"I think it might be good for you to participate in the interviews," Dr. Smith encouraged. "That might shed light on how Cpl. Poole's relating to the students."

"It will be hard to fit in the interviews with my schedule," Dr. Demitri responded, "but I'll see if I can do it."

"That's a good start," Dr. Smith concluded. "You talk with her. I will continue to encourage placements."

Later that day Dr. Demitri called Cpl. Poole to discuss her concerns about the placements. "Maybe I could help interview the students and we can compare notes, just to make sure everything is fitting together," she offered.

"I guess," Cpl. Poole replied.

*I don't know what to think about her. I just know I need some students*, thought Dr. Demitri.

Over the next two weeks, Dr. Demitri spoke to Cpl. Poole about the upcoming semester. Dr. Demitri presented the new syllabus and learning objectives for the MSW field students. Cpl. Poole did not share any concerns, but Dr. Demitri noted that she seemed distracted.

"This has been confusing to me," Dr. Demitri shared with Dr. Smith. "I have offered to help Cpl. Poole, but she doesn't seem that interested in things, one way or another. I really need to test this structured intervention, but I just don't know if she is on board."

The Field Education Office continued to encourage students to consider COMPASS, and Dr. Demitri continued to help Cpl. Poole interview students. One of the students who applied was Lisa Adams, a white applicant with a BSW. Lisa had not met the academic requirements for the advanced-standing cohort and was entering the MSW program as a two-year full-time student. The office described COMPASS as a placement option at the generalist level (not the advanced-generalist level), and Lisa expressed a desire to be a part of it.

A few days later Dr. Demitri and Cpl. Poole interviewed Lisa for COMPASS. "Tell us a little about yourself," Cpl. Poole instructed.

"Well," Lisa said with a shrug, "I'm really not even sure why I'm here. I mean, I want to be in medical social work. I just came to this interview because I was referred by the field office."

*What?* Dr. Demitri wondered. *What does she mean she doesn't know why she's here? I thought the field office said Lisa was interested in the COMPASS Program.*

"Well, let us tell you about it, and see what you think." Dr. Demitri described the students' responsibility in COMPASS, and Cpl. Poole explained the role of the MSW students with the SRO Program. Lisa fielded most of their questions well, and the interview lasted over an hour.

"I'm sorry," Lisa said as she rose to leave. "I don't think my responses were very good. I hope I didn't bomb this too much. Thanks for meeting with me." Lisa smiled nervously. "I am really hoping to be a part of this."

Dr. Demitri pondered. *She doesn't seem very confident. First, she said she was interested in medical social work, and then she said she was interested in COMPASS. She interviewed well, and then she said she thought she bombed it. It is really hard to read her . . . if she does want to be a part of this, it's hard to tell. We need students who will make a real commitment to this placement!*

After Lisa left, Cpl. Poole and Dr. Demitri debriefed. "I have some mixed feelings," Dr. Demitri said. "I don't want to choose someone who isn't going to be a good fit. What do you think?"

Cpl. Poole shrugged. "Well, she answered all the questions, and she seems like she wants to succeed. I kind of like her. I can see her working with sixth-grade students. I think she might be a good fit."

"Does she seem like she is able to make a commitment to this program?"

"What do we have to lose? We have to pick someone," Cpl. Poole responded.

As she left the Cpl. Poole's office, Dr. Demitri thought, *I really want this to work. I hope she is right. Hopefully, Lisa will be a good fit.*

The entire vetting process took over four weeks, and it was close to the beginning of the semester before everything was completed. Finally, Dr. Smith reported, "Lisa made it through. She passed the background, drug screen, and polygraph tests." Dr. Demitri breathed a sigh of relief because the new program was able to go forward with Lisa and the other MSW students.

## COMPASS TRAINING: DAY ONE

The first day of training was scheduled for the next week. Dr. Demitri and Cpl. Poole held a group session with Lisa and the other three students assigned to the COMPASS Program. Everyone made introductions, and Dr. Demitri and Cpl. Poole presented the intervention and reviewed the role of the MSW students. The day went fairly well, and Lisa participated actively in the group discussions.

"Well, I think that went pretty well for a first day. You know, it looks like things are going to work out," assured Cpl. Poole.

*That's the first time she has sounded positive about the new program,* Dr. Demitri thought. *Maybe things are back on track!*

## COMPASS TRAINING: DAY TWO

On the second day of training, all of the students arrived on time except Lisa, who arrived fifteen minutes late. "Well," Cpl. Poole said, acknowledging Lisa, "now that everyone is here, let's go around and have everyone share a little bit more about themselves. We want a chance for everyone to get to know each other better. Lisa, why don't you start?"

"I don't really even want to be here," Lisa began, laughing softly. "You know, I don't know why I'm here. I really didn't want to be in this placement. I wanted to be in medical social work . . . but, well"—Lisa shrugged—"I guess I'm here."

*What's going on now?* Dr. Demitri wondered. *Why would Lisa say that? Why would she keep saying that . . . and why does she keep shrugging? This is the second time she has said that she doesn't want to be in this placement. I need to ask her whether she really wants to be a part of COMPASS. When we have a break, I am going to speak with her.*

During the lunch break, Dr. Demitri spoke with Lisa privately. "Lisa, you've made some statements that make me wonder if you really want this placement."

Lisa looked into Dr. Demitri's eyes and responded, "I'm here, aren't I?"

"Being here isn't enough," Dr. Demitri answered. "This is an important program with a new intervention. I need the MSW students to be committed to COMPASS . . . and I am a little nervous because you said earlier you are not sure you even want to be here. As a matter of fact, you've said it twice. I am wondering what you would think if you were in my shoes."

Lisa was silent for a moment, and tears began to well in her eyes. "I can understand why you might feel that way," Lisa replied, "but I really do want to be here. I want to do well. I do want to be a part of this, of COMPASS."

Following the conversation, Dr. Demitri found herself feeling better about Lisa's desire to participate in COMPASS. Lisa engaged off and on throughout the remainder of the day and sometimes seemed disconnected. She didn't participate in the ongoing conversation, and when class was over, she left quickly without saying a word.

At the end of the day after the students had left, Cpl. Poole approached Dr. Demitri. "You know, Lisa didn't really seem interested at all today. That isn't a good sign. I think I may have been wrong about her. Maybe we should just fire her and find somebody else."

"I had the same concerns, but I spoke to her during lunch. I think she may just be a little overwhelmed, and she is technically a first-year student. It isn't fair of us to expect the same of her as we would of an advanced-practice student," Dr. Demitri offered. "She told me she really does want to be a part of this, and I felt she was very genuine and authentic in our conversation. Let's see what happens tomorrow."

"We don't have a lot of tomorrows before the program starts," Cpl. Poole retorted.

"She's a student. She's learning. She told me she wants to do well in COMPASS," Dr. Demitri replied. As she walked down the hall of the substation, Dr. Demitri could not help but think, *Oh, I hope this works, and this is a matter of managing professional expectations. Cpl. Poole is right—we don't have a lot of tomorrows, but I would hate to give up on a student before she had a chance to even begin.*

## COMPASS TRAINING: DAY THREE

Lisa arrived on time for the third day of training but continued to appear disconnected. She did not participate in the conversation unless asked a direct question, and she texted on her cell phone several times during the morning.

Cpl. Poole approached Dr. Demitri at the break. "You know, this just isn't going to work. Lisa isn't listening. She isn't engaged. She's paying more attention to her phone than anything we are saying. If she's not interested in the training, how can we expect her to be interested in the students?"

"Yes, I noticed Lisa's behavior, too," Dr. Demitri answered. "I really want to give Lisa a chance, though. She's a student. She's in the MSW program to learn, but . . ."

"But what?" Cpl. Poole asked.

"We have already invested a lot of time in her," Dr. Demitri said, "and she's only been here a few days. This is a learning environment for the MSW students, and this is only the training. She hasn't even begun her placement."

Cpl. Poole shook her head and shrugged. "In my experience with this program, sometimes it's just better to cut your losses."

"I know you have been with the practicum longer than I have," Dr. Demitri began. "I value your opinion and your experience. Don't we have as much responsibility to the students of the university as we do to the students in the sixth grade?"

"Of course," Cpl. Poole answered. "This program is to help the MSW students and the kids, but . . ."

"But what?" Dr. Demitri asked.

"But if Lisa is already disconnected before we're even asking her to really begin, what is the likelihood that she is going to be engaged with the students when they really need her? That's what you are really wanting, right? For the MSW students to engage with the at-risk kids? To make a difference in their lives?"

"I hear what you are saying," Dr. Demitri said. "I just don't think it sends the right message to give up on someone before she even has a chance to start. What does that say about our commitment to the learning process, especially for people like Lisa, who need a little more help with the learning process?"

"Listen, I know Lisa is off to a rocky start. I get it, but what makes you think she's going to be successful, anyway? She isn't confident. She isn't interested. She isn't engaged . . . and if we wait until the end of the semester to terminate her, which seems likely, won't that just be harder for her? Not every person is right for every placement," said Cpl. Poole.

"And what about the other students?" Dr. Demitri asked. "What does it say to them if we fire their classmate before the placement even begins? How can we create a positive learning environment if we don't allow our students to learn?"

Cpl. Poole looked at Dr. Demitri and shrugged. "Well, people get fired all the time. But it's your program," she sighed. "I think we should have a meeting, just the three of us."

As Dr. Demitri walked down the hallway, she reflected about how difficult the placement selection process had been. *I'm just not sure what is right*, she pondered. *One day Beth is for Lisa; the next day she isn't. Maybe she's right. Then, again, shouldn't we be responsible for educating students on how their professional conduct impacts practice and how they can improve?*

# 9

# CONFLICTED LEARNERS

*Melissa C. Reitmeier and Terry A. Wolfer*

As the students' group supervision session concluded, Jane Sumpter, their field instructor, couldn't help but notice Shakeita DuBard's face fall in response to Mindy Johnson's comments.

"Shakeita, is everything okay?" Jane asked, prompting Shakeita to pause before exiting the room.

"Everything is great!" Shakeita said with her typical smile and soft voice as she resumed walking.

Jane didn't believe her, and Jane's expression likely said so.

However, another intern, Brittany Davis, hung back, waiting for everyone else to filter out.

---

This decision case was prepared solely to provide material for class discussion and not to suggest either effective or ineffective handling of the situation depicted. While based on field research regarding an actual situation, names and certain facts may have been disguised to protect confidentiality. The authors wish to thank the case reporter for cooperation in making this account available for the benefit of social work students and practitioners.

"Jane?" Brittany said, her tone serious.

"Yes, Brittany?"

"You know, Jane . . . er, um . . . the, the reason that Shakeita is unhappy is because I've heard that Mindy takes over their group and runs the whole thing. She is kind of sweet about it, but she dominates everything. All Shakeita does is hand out lollipops at the end. They talk about it every week," Brittany revealed, lowering her eyes, "but don't say I told you."

Jane felt her face flush as memories of the past few weeks tumbled through her mind.

## YOUNG WOMEN'S CHRISTIAN ASSOCIATION

Incorporated in Texas in 1907 as the Young Women's Christian Association (YWCA) of the University of Texas, the YWCA of Greater Austin now included more than exercise and fitness programs. It was a service organization that focused on the health and human service needs of women and girls, most of whom had low to moderate incomes. It also provided numerous opportunities for social work internships in after-school mentoring and tutoring programs, girls' empowerment groups, teen pregnancy prevention, science programs for girls, and the recently funded Women's Empowerment Program (WEP).

Implemented in the Austin City Jail, WEP provided six weekly, two-hour modules on psychoeducational skills for parenting and self-care to incarcerated mothers of preschool children. In response to the high demand, the YWCA began running two WEP groups simultaneously. Given the turnover in the jail population, as one of the two groups ended, the leaders could start another. Student interns were attracted to this type of group work, too.

## JANE SUMPTER, YWCA PROGRAM DIRECTOR

Jane Sumpter was a licensed independent clinical social worker and the program director for several YWCA programs, including WEP. Jane received her MSW from the University of North Dakota in Grand Forks and had additional intensive training in cognitive behavioral therapy. She had eight years of practice experience in hospice, social services, and private practice and had spent four years with the YWCA. Committed to interns, she had worked with more than thirty of them before moving to Austin, Texas. There she began working as a field instructor for MSW students from the University of Texas at Austin and for BSW students from St. Edward's University. She was white and thirty-five years old, and her wavy, blonde hair rested just below her shoulders. She was soft-spoken, thoughtful, articulate, and bright.

## SOCIAL WORK INTERN COHORT

In February 2006, in preparation for the following academic year, Jane rigorously interviewed several students and settled on six for the fall semester.

The first was Mindy Johnson, a white, thirty-nine-year-old, nontraditional student enrolled in the foundation year of the MSW program at the University of Texas at Austin. She came to social work with a doctorate in religious studies from Boston University and wanted to work one-on-one with individuals, so she sought social work practice experience and a degree that would allow her to do so.

The second foundation-year MSW student was Gertrude Smith, a twenty-seven-year-old African American who appeared interested but shy. As a psychology undergraduate at the University of Texas at Austin, she had maintained a 4.0 GPA.

The third foundation-level MSW student was Brittany Davis, a twenty-five-year-old white woman who was especially extroverted. She and Gertrude went through the psychology program together, finishing at the same time and applying for the MSW program together.

The fourth intern was Shakeita DuBard, an African American who was nearly twenty years of age and a BSW student from St. Edward's University. To Jane, she appeared exceptionally shy and reserved. Shakeita was of average height with short hair and a ready smile.

The final two interns were African American women, one twenty-four and the other twenty-five, in the advanced year of the MSW program. They interned on different days of the week than the other interns and ran a separate after-school group with Brittany. However, all six students met with Jane for group supervision once a week.

The women shared office space that was separated by a portable divider from the conference area/break room where they met for supervision. They also shared a field liaison, Michael Green, a middle-aged white man

## THE FIELD PLACEMENT START-UP FOR WEP: MID-AUGUST

Although the six students engaged in other programs and tasks and had individualized learning contracts, they had shared learning experiences with the WEP and after-school groups. When they started in August, Jane provided a thorough orientation for the group, as she would for any employee. They learned the policies and procedures of the YWCA, as well as the guiding principles of each of the programs in which they would participate. Jane required that all students shadow her the first six weeks to observe her running these psychoeducational groups before coleading the WEP groups.

Jane assigned the students to work in triads for the group leadership portion of their internships. The first group teamed Shakeita, Mindy, and Gertrude. The second group teamed Brittany with the two advanced-practice students because she could participate on the days they were in placement. Jane asked that one be responsible for the opener, another for the lesson, and the third for the closing exercise at their weekly sessions. This leadership was to rotate from week to week, so that everyone had several chances to lead each of the segments. Because Jane had already been through the curriculum and modeled the process, in supervision they focused on discussing group dynamics and issues—specifically, what went well and what didn't—and on planning for the next week.

## FLYING SOLO BEGINNING GROUP

In mid-October, the second installation of the six-week module for WEP began, and all six interns co-led their first group. When time came for weekly supervision, they gathered around the conference table. "Well," Jane opened, "I'm anxious to hear how your first group sessions went this week. Who would like to go first? What happened in WEP this week?"

"Oh, my goodness," Mindy responded immediately. "In the middle of our lesson, one of our clients, Grace, started saying 'They are going to kill me!' " Mindy imitated breathily, " 'They are going to kill me!' and she was pointing to the guards over and over. And then she lay down on the floor and started bawling her eyes out. I was *mortified* and didn't know what to do! It was a wild first group, Jane." Visibly anxious and distraught, Mindy picked at her fingernails.

"I know we need to start where the client is," Gertrude chuckled with a sort of grand patience, "but we *really* didn't know what to do in that situation. This didn't happen during the first six weeks when we watched you, Jane."

Jane glanced toward Shakeita, and Shakeita grimaced. "I didn't say or do a thing," she said, her voice barely audible as she lowered her eyes.

*I'm glad Gertrude seemed to take that in stride*, Jane observed, *but Mindy and Shakeita, not so much.* "Well, what did you do? What happened?"

"Well, we tried to reason with Grace," Mindy said, "but that didn't work, as she was in psychosis or something . . . she can't just take over the group, you know?!" Then her voice trailed off.

"That's right, Mindy. That's a good point," Gertrude said, glancing sideways at one of the other interns.

"But then we just called a guard to remove her," Mindy continued urgently, "because we have to think of the whole group and not just one person." A look of pride flickered across her face.

A group discussion ensued over ways to handle this differently in the future and to uphold integrity for all in a group whether it is psychoeducational or therapeutic. Afterward, Jane walked away thinking, *This is really an excellent group of students. We're really diving into how to put what they're learning in the classroom into practice, especially for groups!*

## THE MIDDLE PHASE

The next two weeks went according to plan, and group supervision followed its usual agenda, with the students processing how the groups were going at the women's jail and the after-school program. It was typical to analyze the group dynamics each week and define what went well and what didn't. Supervision concluded with establishing the lesson plans for the respective groups the interns ran for the next week.

During the week of Halloween, Jane again thought supervision had gone well. But when she left the session, she forgot her cell phone and had to return to the group room to retrieve it. From behind the partition, she could hear someone who sounded like Gertrude saying to someone "It doesn't matter what we do, girl. Mindy will just take it all over. She tells us she is our 'mom,' for goodness sakes. It won't matter at all." And then there was a deep silence, as if they sensed someone was in the conference room.

*What are they talking about?* Jane momentarily panicked. *Mindy butting in? What's going on? Should I ask them if anything is going on? Nobody is saying that anything is wrong.* Not inclined to intervene in personal matters, Jane decided to sleep on it. *Besides*, she thought, *I ask them a million times if they need anything, and maybe this is a personality issue they need to work out.*

The next morning, reflecting on the situation, Jane concluded, *Part of being a professional is asking for help. I'm going to let them struggle with it and let them ask me for help if they need it.*

At the next group supervision, all seemed well, and everyone was laughing, sharing pictures from Halloween, and making plans to go to dinner at the end of the day. *I'm glad I didn't involve myself in potentially idle gossip*, Jane mused, *and ruin their friendly dynamics.*

## TEARS AND A PHONE CALL

The next week, as Jane rounded the corner in the intern office space, she found Shakeita crying in her chair.

"What's going on, Shakeita? What's wrong?" Jane inquired, pulling up a chair to sit down.

"I am just fine." Through sniffles, Shakeita looked at Jane and said, "I am just having a *really* bad day, and I really don't want to talk about it."

Not wanting to pressure her to share something personal, Jane offered, "Why don't you take the afternoon off and just engage in some self-care. Sometimes we all just need a break."

The next day Jane received a call from Michael.

"Hi, Jane. How are you? It's Michael Green. Look, I know we just completed our liaison visit, but Shakeita reached out to me yesterday afternoon with some concerns after you told her to take the afternoon off, and I think it would be a good idea if we all met."

"Of course," Jane replied, surprised by the call and afraid she might be in trouble. "I sensed there may be some issues, but Shakeita didn't share any of her concerns with me when I asked."

## THE MEETING

Michael, Shakeita, and Jane met the next day. Jane was a bit perplexed because she had been asking Shakeita how she was doing, but Shakeita had declined to open up or ask for help. After some pleasantries, Michael turned to the task at hand. "Shakeita came to me because she feels her shyness is getting in the way of her asking for what she needs in placement and she doesn't feel like she's doing much. Right, Shakeita?"

Jane sat back, feeling even more confused. *I know you're shy, but you present in group supervision as if you all are engaging as a team.*

"I just don't feel like I am doing much here," Shakeita confessed. "I think being shy is getting in my way, and I don't know what to do about that or if I can do anything about that."

"Well, Shakeita," Jane said, "I'm glad you brought this to our attention. Let's talk about how we can make sure you have a voice . . . and an opportunity."

Shakeita nodded.

"Is there anything that could be done differently," Jane asked, "that I could help you with?"

"It's just me, I think," Shakeita countered. "I will step it up. I will check in with you in a week. Honestly, I feel better just sharing with you how I am feeling in terms of my shyness and not knowing how to speak up sometimes."

After a bit more conversation, the meeting ended with Shakeita committing to try harder. Although they did not come up with a formal plan, Shakeita said she would inform Jane of specific instances when she could not speak up so they could address those instances in the moment.

*What am I missing?*" Jane puzzled. *She seems completely fine now with her usual smile. Maybe she needs more one-on-one time with me to develop her confidence. I will be sure to keep an eye on her, but I wonder if something else is going on.*

## A DOORKNOB CONFESSION

The following week, as they wrapped up group supervision, Jane took in the glorious moment: all six of her social work interns were engaged in a warm and lively conversation, discussing their upcoming Thanksgiving plans. *This is the best group of students I've ever had,* Jane mused, *and I'm so excited about all the real social work they're doing.* Jane hated to interrupt the moment but said, "I'm here if you need to discuss anything this next week. Remember I'm always available to meet with you one-on-one. Enjoy your last group before your short break."

"I really think that the opener is *key* for the content next week," Mindy said with a self-assured tone as she pointed to the handouts Jane provided.

Jane thought she caught an eye roll from Gertrude, which elicited giggles from Brittany, Melody, and Krystal, but maybe she had missed something. "And then the closer will be relaxation!" Mindy emphasized as she gazed at her co-leaders.

Jane couldn't help but notice Shakeita's face fall in response to Mindy's comments as the student group supervision concluded.

"Shakeita, is everything okay?" Jane asked, prompting Shakeita to pause before exiting the room.

"Everything is great!" Shakeita said with her typical smile and soft voice as she resumed walking.

Jane didn't believe her, and Jane's expression likely said so.

However, Brittany hung back, waiting for everyone else to filter out.

"Jane?" Brittany said, her tone serious.

"Yes, Brittany?"

"You know, Jane . . . er, um . . . the, the reason that Shakeita is unhappy is because I've heard that Mindy takes over their group and runs the whole thing. She is kind of a sweet about it, but she dominates everything. All Shakeita does is hand out lollipops at the end. They talk about it every week," Brittany revealed, lowering her eyes, "but don't say I told you."

Jane felt her face flush as memories of the past few weeks tumbled through her mind. Perplexed, she wondered, *Why is no one saying anything to me? Brittany is not even a part of their triad, so how does she know? Are they all discussing it behind Mindy's back? Shakeita didn't bring this up when we met with the liaison. How do I intervene? Do I even intervene? Should I address this and rescue Shakeita? Do I betray Brittany's confidence? What do I do?*

# 10

## NO WAY TO DRIVE

*Melissa C. Reitmeier and Terry A. Wolfer*

Field instructor Chris Ebert checked his calendar for the week and noted that he needed to prepare for an appointment later that afternoon. He was scheduled to meet with Sharon Johnson, a field liaison who also served as the university's field director, and his BSW student, Beth Mathis. *I have NO idea how to approach this meeting.* Chris sighed with exasperation. *Should I tell Sharon what is going on, or do I keep my mouth shut? I certainly don't want to throw Beth under the bus, but I've already talked to her about this.* A wave of guilt washed over him as he remembered the key events leading up to discussing her work with clients and then confronting her.

---

This decision case was prepared solely to provide material for class discussion and not to suggest either effective or ineffective handling of the situation depicted. While based on field research regarding an actual situation, names and certain facts may have been disguised to protect confidentiality. The authors wish to thank the case reporter for cooperation in making this account available for the benefit of social work students and practitioners.

During their supervisory session the week before, he had pleaded with her. "Let's come clean about this," Chris said softly but intently. "Let's talk it through. This is impacting your work with our clients."

Unresponsive, Beth sat perfectly still, but then her petite frame wilted a bit, and her eyes turned downward. "No, that's okay. It's *not* a problem. I mean, I am and have been doing the *best* I can," she said as she raised her eyes to meet Chris's eyes, "given the circumstances."

## SALVATION ARMY

The Salvation Army of Vermillion, South Dakota, was a part of the organization's western division and was established over one hundred years ago. The Salvation Army was an evangelical part of the universal Christian Church, and its message was based on the Bible. Its ministry was motivated by the love of God, and its mission was to preach the gospel of Jesus Christ and to meet human needs in his name without discrimination. Although its roots were religious, many did not associate its faith-based message with the social services it provided in the community. Viewed as a needed social service entity in Vermillion, it provided a broad range of programs and services that included material assistance programs (e.g., food, clothing, and utilities), restorative and therapeutic services for community members, and permanent subsidized housing for aging residents (those aged fifty-five and older) with disabilities.

The Salvation Army was awarded a grant in partnership with the Vermillion Housing Authority to provide case management services to residents of its subsidized housing program. Unfortunately, the previous decade had been fraught with high turnover because residents had violated housing policy (e.g., engaging in drug and substance use and other crimes). The newly funded case management program, packaged as a wraparound program, was designed to address these issues and improve housing outcomes for residents. The organization quickly hired all personnel required to launch the program: two BSW-level case managers; an MSW therapist, Rebecca Shevsky; and a program director, Chris Ebert.

## CHRIS EBERT, PROGRAM DIRECTOR

Chris Ebert was a thirty-seven-year-old, white man. He began his social work education five years earlier at the University of Southern California. About a year and a half after graduating with an MSW, he moved to Vermillion and began practicing social work at the South Dakota AIDS Project. He was often described as a kind and earnest social worker, always the person at the table who took a strengths-based perspective when solving problems or discussing difficult situations. This approach earned him great respect among colleagues, and he was often touted as the most compassionate practitioner in the group. It also explained why the University of South Dakota, located in Vermillion, appreciated his service as a field instructor for several social work students.

After a few years at the AIDS Project, a great job opportunity offered Chris the chance to expand his administrative skill set. The new program director job for the Salvation Army was ideal for someone with his deep passion for and practice experience in working with people who were homeless and managing mental health needs, and he quickly applied.

## REBECCA SHEVSKY, BEHAVIOR INTERVENTIONIST

Rebecca Shevsky was a twenty-five-year-old, white woman. A recent graduate of Portland State University's MSW program, she specialized in mental health. She had just obtained her advanced LISW-CP license after practicing at a local community-based mental health center for two years. She dressed professionally yet stylishly, and this made for a dramatic contrast with her clients. Rebecca came across as highly competent, although older colleagues viewed her as a bit entitled. She was on the fast track even though she did not have as much direct practice experience as other colleagues on the grant. She was a first-time field preceptor and eager to prove her worth as a supervisor.

## SHARON JOHNSON, FIELD DIRECTOR AND FIELD LIAISON

Sharon Johnson was a forty-five-year-old, African American woman who had served as the director of field education at the University of South Dakota for ten years. She had obtained her MSW from the University of Wyoming when she was twenty-three and had been a practicing family services social worker with the Department of Social Services for twelve years before becoming the director of field education. Sharon was poised and impeccably dressed at all times but not always planful or considerate of other people's time. Although she always got students placed for field, she often did so at the last minute by leaning on field instructors.

## PREPARING FOR STUDENT INTERNS

Before starting the new job, Chris notified the field program at the University of South Dakota that he would be transitioning to a new place of employment. Sharon quickly asked about student field opportunities at the new agency. Chris responded, "I'm not sure. Let me check on that, and I will get back to you."

During Chris's first week on the job, the phone rang, and Chris picked it up, only to be greeted by Sharon's raspy yet assertive voice on the other end.

"Hey, Chris. I hope your first week is going well. Listen," Sharon's said, her voice turning serious, "I have two interns that I need to place like right away! We are having some struggles, and you have the perfect disposition to mentor them. Would you be willing to take them on?"

*I don't know what she's getting me into*, Chris thought. *I know there's a reason these students have not been placed yet.* But he responded, "Well, I don't have interns, and we could use the help, especially now that I see the range of social work practice opportunities. Sure, Sharon. I'll take them on." *Maybe*, Chris reassured himself, *these students just need a fresh opportunity, and we can learn this job together.*

In late August, Chris held the first meeting with the two students, both of whom were pursuing a BSW in the College of Social Work. Beth Mathis was white, twenty-three years of age, and a petite 5'4". Charles Winston was white and twenty-five years of age and had been diagnosed with mild cerebral palsy. He walked with a limp, displayed a limited range of motion in his gait, and spoke with a bit of a slur when excited.

After meeting the students, Chris quickly appointed preceptors. He paired Beth with Rebecca and Charles with one of the new BSW case managers. During the meeting, Chris did not note anything special or out of the ordinary with either student and felt more confident about his decision to take students on short notice.

After the students left the first meeting, however, Rebecca observed, "My, Beth looks like she's had it rough. . . . Likely drugs."

"No," Chris countered, "she looks like she has lived a full life to be only twenty-three." But he had to admit that the network of visible tattoos splattered across her pale arms and legs left him wondering what her "story" was. As he liked to say, "Everyone has a story."

## THE FIELD PLACEMENT START-UP

The first week of field for both students went smoothly. They shadowed their preceptors and began jumping in where needed.

During the second week, Chris was sitting in his office when the phone rang. "Hello, this is Chris Ebert. How can I help you today?"

"Chris, this is Rebecca." Her voice was urgent. "I asked Beth to take one of our female residents—er, um, clients—to an appointment across town this morning."

There was a pregnant pause.

"And?" Chris inquired softly.

"Well," Rebecca stammered, "she, she got into a car accident with the client."

"Is everyone okay?" Chris asked calmly.

"It appears so. They're being checked right now, but," Rebecca added, "Beth's car looks pretty bad."

"Okay," Chris paused, his head spinning. "Well, you stay with them, and I will call my supervisor and see what we need to do in terms of protocol and insurance."

## WHO'S RESPONSIBLE?

Because Frank Clinton, the executive director, was tough to reach—always attending a meeting or managing various grant projects—Chris was surprised when he answered his cell phone on the first try.

"Frank Clinton here," a firm voice projected over the phone.

"Hi, Frank. It's Chris Ebert." Chris paused, unsure how his new boss would react to this type of situation. "One of the interns on our grant got into a car accident with one of our clients. They were on the way to an appointment. No one is hurt, but since I'm new, I'm not sure of the next steps or the protocol we should follow."

"Salvation Army has an insurance department for things like this. Look it up in the company directory," Frank advised, "and let me know what they say. Keep me posted."

*Okay*, Chris thought, as he sat down at his desk, bracing himself for a series of exchanges to manage any risk and liability that might be barreling his way. *I should let Sharon know what is going on, too.* He reached the insurance department and explained why he was calling and concluded with "Nobody got hurt, but the student's car is damaged."

After being placed on hold, Chris sent an email to Sharon to let her know what was happening. Just as he sent the email, the insurance department clicked back on.

"Mr. Ebert, Mr. Ebert, are you there? What was the student's name again? We can't find any records that a Beth Mathis completed any insurance papers for driving clients on behalf of the Salvation Army. When was her employee start date?"

"She's not an employee." Chris felt pressure in the pit of his stomach. "She's a student intern."

"Well, Mr. Ebert, we don't allow volunteers, which I believe your student would qualify as, to drive clients . . . unless they complete additional paperwork which requires a signed release so we can access their driving records. Technically, this student and her car are not covered under our insurance policies."

"Oh, okay," Chris responded.

*Surely the Salvation Army with all of its donations and money would pay for replacing her car*—Chris's head started spinning again—*or fixing it. It's not like it was a Lexus; it was an old Ford Tempo.*

Chris quickly called Frank back. Frank must have recognized Chris's number because he answered with "Yep. Go on."

Chris explained what he had just learned and encouraged Frank to consider how they might help the student out if her car needed to be repaired.

"Hmmm." Frank paused. "Well, this is a *really* unfortunate situation but"—he paused again—"she *really* shouldn't have been driving in the first place, so there is nothing we can formally do for her. There would be no way to financially cover that, as we don't have a line item for that type of expense. . . . Which reminds me, be sure that you give me a final report on everything, and we can touch base in the morning."

Before Chris left work that day, he confirmed that no one was injured, told Rebecca what Frank had said, and talked with Sharon. As stated in the field manual, Sharon confirmed that the university did not insure students who chose to drive their own vehicle to transport clients. She also said she specifically discouraged this during field orientation. Although relieved that no one was hurt, Chris felt especially concerned when Beth called him right before he left work that day.

"Hi, Chris," Beth began. "So I guess you know what happened?" Without waiting for a response, she continued. "Rebecca told me that Salvation Army won't cover my car damage. I don't think that's right, since I was asked to transport Salvation Army clients." Her voice trembled when she said, "The guy said my car looked totaled when they towed it off," and then became almost inaudible as she followed with, "I won't be able to get anywhere!"

"I know," Chris said. "I am so sorry." After a brief pause, Chris continued. "Apparently, you would have needed to complete that optional paperwork provided to you during orientation to qualify for coverage under Salvation Army's insurance policy. Since that didn't happen, your car is not covered."

Silence ensued on the other end of the phone.

Chris continued cautiously. "Why don't you take the next day or even a few days off to recoup from this and to figure out a transportation plan for reentry to field?"

"Okay, but I could afford only liability car insurance. I don't have collision on my car. I am strapped financially and uncertain what I can do other than walk to class and field, which is a great distance . . . or maybe I could take public transit."

"That sounds like a good plan. Very proactive, Beth." Chris tried to be positive, but he felt awkward and inadequate. "Let me know what you find out."

"Okay," Beth responded. "I will talk to you next week."

## THE NEXT MORNING

Back in the office, Chris had just grabbed his coffee and was zipping through morning emails, catching up after the incident yesterday, which had required so much of his time and attention. When the phone rang, he answered with "Good morning!"

"Is it?" Rebecca barked angrily on the other end.

*Apparently, she's been stewing all night*, Chris thought.

"I heard what you told Beth." Rebecca forged ahead. "That is the most ridiculous thing. Can't you do anything? Make Frank do something!" Rebecca ranted. "You should be able to fix this, Chris. You're the program director!"

*You didn't consult me before advising Beth to transport the client!* Chris mused, *YOU are partially, if not largely, responsible for this situation. But that wouldn't be very productive at this point*. Chris checked himself. *No, I'm the program director. It falls on me to make sure things like this do not happen. I should know these policies and am ultimately responsible for the interns. I know you're just aligning yourself with Beth.*

"Well, Rebecca," Chris finally interjected, "the insurance department argues that the fault resides with the student for not completing paperwork as a volunteer. According to them, she was provided these options during agency orientation but did not complete them. I'm sure this is likely because they were listed as optional during the prerequisite process. Technically, Salvation Army has no way to allocate funds to help her. Our hands are tied."

## THE NEXT WEEK

When Beth returned to placement the following week, Chris sat down to talk with her right away.

"Let's talk about the car situation, Beth. Last we spoke, you were really upset with me and Salvation Army. I want you to know that I'm not in agreement with this either, but technically the paperwork was not in place to cover you on our end. You have every right to your emotional experience, so let's process this."

"I know there is nothing you can do." Beth looked him in the eye. "I am just struggling without having a car." Sighing, she continued, "It takes three times as long to get from one place to another using public transit and it wears on me emotionally . . . it impacts my schedule. But I am *fine*." Her voice and face expressionless, she asserted, "I'm over it and understand."

*I'm not buying this*, Chris thought, *but I'm not sure if I should push the issue today. Maybe with time, things will improve.* "Alright, Beth. Please know that I am always available to discuss this further. Let's move on to discussing the clients we are pairing you with for the next few weeks."

## THE FOLLOWING WEEKS

Beth attended as usual during the first week after the accident, but then she started to call in, not show up, or show up on different days over the next three weeks. She would always inform Rebecca that it was because of transportation. Then Rebecca called Chris to report some new developments.

"Chris, I hesitated calling you last week about this, but I think I need to let you know something now—before it gets worse."

"Sure, Rebecca," Chris responded. "How can I help?"

"I've had several residents tell me they do not want to work with Beth. They describe her as hostile and rude. And to be quite honest, she doesn't seem to be able to really engage with them. I've observed her for two sessions, and it's been quite the challenge. Cognitively, she just doesn't seem to be very invested in the 'relationship' part of the therapeutic process. She talks a lot about where she is with field hours, like she is just clocking them, and she doesn't seem focused on the 'learning' part of the field experience."

"Have you talked to her about this?" Chris inquired.

"Yes, I have spoken to her several times, but she *always says* that she's 'just doing the best I can, given the circumstances.' Since the accident, she does come across as an angry person." Rebecca paused. "Chris, she resists feedback and just participates passively. For example, not coming in and being disengaged are just not acceptable. Clients don't want to work with her. This is a new program, and we need for it to be successful. I told her I was going to connect with you so you could discuss this in formal supervision, since she is unwilling to acknowledge there is a problem in her clinical skill set."

"Thanks, Rebecca. I will look into it later today."

*I wonder if there are some unresolved issues regarding the accident. We have held her less accountable in some ways regarding her spotty attendance. I'm not sure if this is related to the accident or,* Chris wondered, *if this may be the reason she was difficult to place to begin with."*

### THE SUPERVISION SESSION

Later that day Chris heard a knock at his door. Beth entered with her notebook and she sat down, her arms crossed.

"Rebecca brought to my attention," Chris began, "some feedback you've received regarding your interactions with clients the last few weeks. Would you like to talk about that?"

"No. Not really. I think I am doing fine. I just started," Beth replied.

"Well, I was wondering if you might be experiencing some resentment toward Salvation Army for your current transportation predicament."

"As you stated," Beth countered, "there is nothing you can do."

"Let's come clean about this," Chris said softly but intently. "Let's talk it through. This is impacting your work with our clients."

Unresponsive, Beth sat perfectly still, but then her petite frame wilted a bit, and her eyes turned downward. "No, that's okay. It's *not* a problem. I mean, I am and have been doing the *best* I can," as she raised her eyes to meet Chris's eyes, "given the circumstances."

*I am glad Rebecca warned me about that line*, Chris thought to himself. "Well, then, Beth, how might we understand the feedback we're receiving from clients? If the accident is not impacting your work with clients, what is getting in the way?"

After several unsuccessful attempts to draw out a discussion, Chris decided to require that Beth complete a process recording of her last awkward interaction with a client who reported Beth was hostile and unfriendly. Chris expected this to be completed by their supervision session the following week. As Chris closed the door behind Beth, he found himself thinking, *I'm starting to struggle with her, too, and she does not seem very invested, just like Rebecca reported.*

## THE MIDSEMESTER FIELD LIAISON VISIT

A week later Chris checked his calendar and noted that he needed to prepare for the midsemester field liaison visit with Sharon and Beth later that afternoon. *I have NO idea how to approach this meeting.* Chris sighed with exasperation. *Should I tell Sharon what is going on, or do I keep my mouth shut? I certainly don't want to throw Beth under the bus, but I've already talked to her about this. Beth should have completed the process recording I assigned, but I'm not certain I should bring that up with Sharon. . . .*

# 11

## HE WON'T GO THERE!

*Maria L. Hogan and Terry A. Wolfer*

In April 2012, field instructor Ellen James and field liaison Julia Cathcart visited Calvin Ellis at his field placement with Champion Academy, an alternative school in Jackson County, Georgia. Before bringing the end-of-year field visit to a close, Julia asked Calvin, "What was your greatest challenge?"

"One night after field," Calvin answered, after a brief pause, "I had to drop by a student's house to make a home visit. I wanted to check on him because he didn't show up to school that day. It was dark when I pulled up and got out of the car. When I got to the door, there was someone standing there with a gun."

---

This decision case was prepared solely to provide material for class discussion and not to suggest either effective or ineffective handling of the situation depicted. While based on field research regarding an actual situation, names and certain facts may have been disguised to protect confidentiality. The authors wish to thank the case reporter for cooperation in making this account available for the benefit of social work students and practitioners.

"What?! Did you call the police?" Ellen asked, incredulous. "What did you do?" *And why*, Ellen wondered, *are you just mentioning this now?! I gave you every opportunity to tell me that this horrible thing happened.* Glancing sideways at Julia, Ellen's mind was racing. *What do we do with this information now?*

## JACKSON COUNTY, GEORGIA, AND CHAMPION ACADEMY

With just over sixty thousand residents, Jackson County's population was over 80 percent white, 12 percent African American, and 7 percent Hispanic. About 13 percent of its residents were below the poverty line, and the county continued to struggle with the effects of the 2008 recession, which had occurred four years earlier. Small impoverished areas were scattered about the county, and crime was rampant. Because of budget cuts, the Jackson County School District had eliminated social work positions, leaving fewer resources to address student problems.

Located in the town of Jefferson, Champion Academy served as Jackson County's alternative school for students expelled from the three other high schools. The academy was going through a transition to make it more therapeutic, which included hiring an on-site psychologist. It had also recently changed its branding by using vibrant colors and renaming the school to instill more positivity. As part of this new branding, the principal broadcast positive affirmations over the PA system throughout the day.

Despite the recent changes, the school building itself remained dark, dirty, and run-down. It was old and very small, and the narrow halls lacked the typical team spirit that tended to fill the hallways in a high school. Security guards stood at the doors, and students were often accompanied by staff as they walked the halls. The academy's census ranged from a few dozen students to more than one hundred students at any given time.

Dr. Christopher Haines, Champion Academy's principal and one of the key people behind the rebranding, was kind, generous, and welcoming. Standing 6'4" tall, he was a fifty-five-year-old white man with blond hair. He always wore khakis, a belt, and a white dress shirt. A long-time educator, he had a passion for working in difficult educational settings, and people perceived him as an innovator.

The academic support staff at the school included Trina Brown, the guidance counselor. She was a quiet, reserved, modestly dressed African American woman in her early sixties. Small in stature, she always appeared proper and hospitable. She had a master's degree in guidance counseling and had worked in the Jackson County School District for twenty-two years. As a guidance counselor, she worked closely with Champion's students to help them plan their futures and overcome obstacles. She missed collaborating with school social workers.

## SOCIAL WORK PLACEMENT

To replace the missing school social workers, Jack Thomas strategized with Kristen Dane. Jack was the dynamic and gregarious fund-raiser, grant writer, and developer for the school district, and Kristen was the dean of the University of Georgia's School of Social Work. Together, they wrote a successful grant proposal to create three new social work field placements for the 2011–2012 school year. Because there were no on-site social workers at Champion, Dean Dane arranged for the School of Social Work's Field Education Office to provide an off-site field instructor for the social work students placed there.

After the grant was awarded, Dr. Haines and a team of staff members interviewed several social work students for the three new field placement positions. Dr. Haines was looking for students who were independent and knowledgeable. He eventually selected Calvin Ellis, an older African American man, and two women in their early twenties, one African American and the other white.

## SCHOOL OF SOCIAL WORK TEAM

The Field Education Office selected Ellen James, a social worker with extensive practice experience, to provide off-site supervision for the social work students at Champion. A forty-eight-year-old white woman, she was about 5'2" tall with short, brown hair. Originally from Georgia, she moved to Chicago to get her MSW from Loyola University. She stayed there for twelve years doing federal grant–funded street outreach with individuals who were experiencing homelessness and who appeared to have mental illnesses, and she developed a strong commitment to social justice and people on the street. In 2008, she returned to Georgia to begin her doctoral program at the University of Georgia's School of Social Work. While taking classes, Ellen also worked for the Region 2 office of the Department of Mental Health, funded by the same grant as her Chicago position.

In 2011, Ellen left her job at the Department of Mental Health to focus her time in the academic setting. She earned income and reduced tuition by teaching two classes per semester and providing field instruction while she worked on her dissertation. Though she had been the field instructor for one student at the Department of Mental Health, she became an off-site field instructor for the first time when she took on the three students placed with Champion Academy.

Ellen worked closely with Julia Cathcart, the field liaison for the Champion Academy social work students. A forty-one-year-old white woman, she had worked with more than twenty-five students as a field instructor. However, this was her first time serving in the role of field liaison. She held an MSW and a PhD in social work and began teaching at the University of Georgia as an adjunct instructor in 2004. Julia and Ellen knew each other from teaching some of the same courses and were both supervised by Dean Dane. Because the Jackson County School District was a new field placement, Ellen and Julia put extra effort into ensuring that they and their field students succeeded.

## CALVIN ELLIS, GRADUATE STUDENT INTERN

Calvin Ellis, a light-skinned African American, was tall, thin, and sixty years of age. He had green eyes, long manicured fingernails, and a gold tooth. He was always meticulously dressed, wearing ironed suits, big rings, and gemstone jewelry, and he always carried a leather folio from his time as a military chaplain. Having earned his master's degree in divinity, he had served as a military chaplain for twenty-five years, and he attended a local church where Trina was a member. Calvin returned to school in 2011 to obtain his MSW from the University of Georgia. As a foundation-year student in the two-year MSW program, Calvin demonstrated great interest in being a leader and maintaining a presence in the College of Social Work. He took part in the dean's advisory council, and he often dropped by a professor's office just to say hello.

Despite his military experience and interest in leadership, Calvin remained without a placement as the fall semester approached. Several agencies interviewed him for a possible placement, but each chose another student. Finally, Calvin interviewed with Champion in July 2011, and Dr. Haines thought his confident, outgoing manner made him the perfect student for the new social work placement.

## GETTING UNDERWAY

When Calvin began his placement, Dr. Haines was assigned to be his task supervisor. Calvin also started meeting with Ellen, the off-site field instructor for all three students.

A few weeks after the placement began, Ellen stopped by Julia's office to give her an update. "The other day I told Calvin that I was working on my dissertation, and he responded, 'Oh, so you're not a professor?' "

"How rude!" Julia responded. "Did he say anything else that seemed odd?"

"Well," Ellen replied, "I've asked him several times why he chose social work, only to get incomplete answers that never quite made sense."

In her role as liaison, Julia checked in with Calvin to see if he needed any help advocating for anything related to developing his learning contract and preparing for his first liaison visit. Julia found that her offer of assistance seemed to open the door for Calvin to stop by and see her spontaneously from time to time throughout the year. Their conversations often followed the same pattern.

"Hi, Dr. Cathcart," Calvin would begin. "I was in the area and thought I would stop by and say hello."

"Hi, Calvin. How is the field placement going?"

"It's going well. I love working with these kids. How are you doing?"

"I'm doing well, Calvin. Thanks for asking."

Typically, this exchange was followed by a pause and a big smile from Calvin. Julia would usually conclude with "Well, I appreciate you stopping by to check in, Calvin."

A couple months later Ellen returned to talk with Julia. "He just seems like a loose cannon to me," Ellen stated.

"Why's that?" Julia probed.

"Every time I meet with him in supervision," Ellen explained, "he hardly participates. It seems like he's keeping information from me, and I never know what to expect with him. He never tells me his feelings or insights. I can't figure out how to rein him in or get him more involved in supervision. It's like he thinks he has everything figured out whenever he comes for supervision and he does not need me to help him along."

"Do you need me to intervene?" Julia asked. "Or meet with the both of you?"

"No," Ellen replied. "I think I'm okay. I just wanted to keep you updated."

As the semester wore on, Ellen tried everything she could think of to get Calvin to engage.

"This is not going to go well," she said to him directly during one meeting, "if you don't respond when I ask you questions."

In response, Calvin nodded his head affirmatively but pushed back from the table without comment.

No matter how hard she tried, it seemed Ellen could not get him to participate in supervision.

On several occasions, without advanced notice, Calvin did not show up for supervision meetings. *How can I do better*, Ellen wondered, *get him better engaged, and get him working harder?* Calvin did not fit her expectations of a social work intern.

While foundation-year social work students often do not know what they are supposed to do in their field settings, Calvin never appeared to hesitate and never expressed uncertainty. In fact, Ellen had to admit that, as best she could tell, he performed competently, meeting expectations for foundation-level performance. He carried out his social work role with confidence, immediately meeting with high school students and building relationships. However, he often called Ellen about technical matters: how he should keep his files, what he should do with his time sheets, and what the rules were about taking client information home. When Calvin raved about his positive feedback from students and staff at Champion, Ellen thought, *I would love to hear what the students have to say about Calvin. He seems severe and conservative.*

As the fall semester progressed, Ellen noticed that Calvin occasionally referenced his military chaplaincy. One day Ellen told the three students she supervised, "All of you are learning to practice social work, and whatever you were before, you have to let that go." Knowing that this directly impacted Calvin, Ellen was surprised that he did not say anything in return. *Most people love that conversation*, Ellen thought. *They want to become social workers. I'm not sure he wants to be a social worker.*

Ellen expressed her concerns about Calvin's chaplaincy to Julia, as she was unsure about his ability to keep an open mind.

Later, when she again raised the issue with Calvin, he responded, "In chaplaincy, you are trained not to be any one religion, but you are well versed in them all, and you take a neutral approach."

Having an ex-husband who was also a military chaplain, Ellen was not convinced. She felt uneasy seeing the gold cross around Calvin's neck and hearing him talk about his wife staying home to cook and clean all day.

Calvin's polite disagreement with her feedback bothered Ellen well into the spring semester. She very much wanted the placement to succeed so this new initiative could continue. She felt honored to be chosen as the field instructor in this new setting, and she wanted to make Dean Dane proud. However, with little response from Calvin, working with him reminded her of working with reluctant clients.

Taking another approach, Ellen tried to involve Calvin with the other two social work students working at Champion Academy, but Calvin never interacted much with them either. Ellen occasionally encouraged them, saying "I really want you guys to bounce ideas off each other." But as far as she knew, it never occurred.

Feeling stymied by Calvin, Ellen stopped by Julia's office and knocked lightly.

"How's it going?" Julia asked

"Good, good," Ellen replied. "It seems like my field students are mostly doing okay, but I have some concerns about Calvin. When we're in supervision, the other two students engage with me and, when I ask, tell me more about what's going on."

"But not Calvin?" Julia guessed.

"Right. When I say something like 'Let's talk a little bit more about that,' they open up, but Calvin typically says, 'That's really all I need.'

I might respond, 'But I want to hear some more. I am concerned about what you said.' But he always shuffles me along with 'No, that's okay. Let's move on.' "

"Do you think it's something that I could help facilitate between you two?" Julia asked.

"No," Ellen replied. "I think it's okay at this point, but thank you for offering. Maybe Calvin just feels difficult by comparison to the other two."

## AN EMAIL FROM DR. HAINES

Ellen and Julia made a joint field visit in late January 2012 to check up on Calvin and the two women at Champion Academy. While students tend to have one field visit per semester, Ellen and Julia liked to make more visits to new placements to make sure the placements were going well, especially placements where social workers were not on-site. During this first spring visit, Calvin mentioned that he was not getting a lot of referrals. Ellen thought that was odd but didn't say anything in the moment.

On the car ride home, Ellen and Julia talked about their concern for Calvin. "Is there something that he's not telling us?" Julia asked.

"I get that feeling, too," Ellen replied. "Calvin used to rave about how many referrals he was getting in the fall, so why is he suddenly not getting quite so many?"

"You're right," Julia responded. "I got a weird feeling that Calvin was not telling us everything. It could be about the referral situation. Has he said anything to you about it or anything else in supervision?"

"No, I haven't heard anything about a lack of referrals," Ellen said, "or much of anything else for that matter. Should I ask him about it?"

"We should probably look into it," Julia stated, "but I don't want Calvin to think that we're questioning him, so let's ask Dr. Haines first to see what he knows about that."

"Maybe it's just a January slump," Ellen offered, "you know, getting back to school after Christmas break."

"Maybe," Julia agreed, "but it seemed like something was off."

When they returned to campus, Ellen emailed Dr. Haines. The next day she received a response:

> Calvin is doing a terrific job. As for the low number of referrals, our census is down from over 100 to just over 30. Maybe a lower number of students is resulting in less referrals to Calvin.

"Interestingly," Ellen reported to Julia a month later, "Calvin has called me several times a week to check in and asked a few small questions. I am glad he's doing that, at least, and want to encourage him to use me more often."

## THE FINAL FIELD VISIT

Having made three prior visits together, Julia and Ellen knew right where to meet for Calvin's final field visit in early April 2012.

"I have just felt so discouraged about my supervisory relationship with Calvin," Ellen confided during the ride there, "and I know you may not want to hear this, but I am just glad that this placement is almost over."

"I know this has been a challenging situation for you this year," Julia responded.

As they drove together, their conversation moved on to another student on the schedule that day and whether they would have enough travel time between the forty-five-minute sessions they had planned with each student.

Calvin was their first visit of the day, and they arrived on time, eager to begin. They both knew what to expect from the visit because the week before Ellen had seen Calvin in supervision and Calvin had stopped by Julia's office as usual to say hello and report that all was going well. Ellen had also been in contact with Dr. Haines, who always reported Calvin was doing a great job.

Calvin had his own office, and students came to him on a regular basis. He had even made himself a name plate and business cards. When Ellen and Julia reached Calvin's office, they found him waiting for them at his desk. Wearing his usual suit, Calvin stood up and shook their hands. Then he went to get Trina and Dr. Haines from nearby offices. They went into the conference room and sat down around the table, with Julia and Ellen on one side, Calvin and Trina on another, and Dr. Haines at the head of the table. After some initial pleasantries, they discussed some therapeutic changes at the school.

"The reason I'm here today," Julia said, turning her attention to Calvin, "is to review your learning contract and progress toward your year-end goals." Julia went through a list of questions that she asked at every field visit, including questions about competency attainment and how classroom learning fit with what Calvin was learning in his placement. She also asked questions about supervision and how it had gone throughout the year. "Are you getting everything that you need from Ellen?"

"Oh, yes, ma'am," Calvin responded. "We've been meeting regularly. Everything's been going okay."

"What about the supervision you're getting here?" Julia probed.

"Oh, yes, ma'am, Trina is always here and we have been working together."

"He's been great with the students," Trina responded. "We're really going to miss him. The students are really going to miss having him here."

Dr. Haines remained quiet through the discussion.

"Ellen," Julia turned to her colleague, "what can you say about Calvin's progress?"

"I've been impressed with what I've heard about Calvin's ability to engage with students," Ellen responded. "I've also been impressed with his professionalism." Because it was the final field visit, Ellen did not want to bring up any negative aspects of supervision. Instead, she tried to think of positive things she could say about Calvin.

Julia continued asking about competencies and termination with clients. As she was beginning to wrap up, she asked Calvin, "Looking back, what do you think was your greatest success?"

"My greatest success has been engaging with the students," Calvin replied. "One student in particular comes to mind. He came to my office often to talk about his awful home life, and I tried to give him hope for his future. A few months ago he went back to the regular high school. I was so excited and encouraged to see him develop his full potential through my work with him. Over the course of the past year, I like to think I helped empower students so they can break the typical cycle of going directly to the Department of Juvenile Justice after leaving Champion."

"That's great!" Julia replied. Before focusing on the transition to next year, she asked, "And what was your greatest challenge?"

"One night after field," Calvin answered, after a brief pause, "I had to drop by a student's house to make a home visit. I wanted to check on him because he didn't show up to school that day. It was dark when I pulled up and got out of the car. When I got to the door, there was someone standing there with a gun. I left and did not get to see the student. It turns out that the student was fine and returned to school the next day. I must have had the wrong address."

"What?! Did you call the police?" Ellen asked, incredulous. "What did you do?" *And why*, Ellen wondered, *are you just mentioning this now?! I gave you every opportunity to tell me that this horrible thing happened*. Glancing sideways at Julia, Ellen's mind was racing. *What do we do with this information now?*

"No," Calvin replied. "I just made sure that I parked in backwards so I would have an easy out. It wasn't a very big deal."

*This is not in your learning contract!* Ellen blushed. *You know you're not supposed to do home visits!* Ellen noticed Julia scan the room and saw Dr. Haines was bug-eyed, apparently surprised. In contrast, Trina appeared unsurprised.

*You misled me!* Ellen felt anger rising, but almost immediately she wondered, *What do I say in front of all of these people?! What are they thinking about me?*

# 12

## PROTECTING CHILDREN

*Sara J. English and Terry A. Wolfer*

Field liaison Mai Le remembered well her time as a field student at the Child Save orphanage in Hanoi and her concern about the way the Child Save Mothers sometimes treated the children. This concern was prompted by what she was learning in her social work program. She thought about her current role as a teacher and liaison and the way her perspective had changed.

She felt caught. Her University of Hanoi field students were upset about similar things they observed in their field placements. So, the day before, Mai had met with the Head Mother at Child Save to discuss their concerns. Today she was to report what happened. As the meeting

---

This decision case was prepared solely to provide material for class discussion and not to suggest either effective or ineffective handling of the situation depicted. While based on field research regarding an actual situation, names and certain facts may have been disguised to protect confidentiality. The authors wish to thank the case reporter for cooperation in making this account available for the benefit of social work students and practitioners.

with the students drew near, Mai wondered what she could say. She knew they were frustrated and eager to make change. They would ask if she had told the Head Mother what was right, if she had been able to correct the Head Mother's thinking.

Now the field students had gathered in the conference room. As she walked down the hall, Mai could hear them talking and whispering to one another. She took a deep breath and entered the room.

## SOCIAL WORK EDUCATION IN VIETNAM

Social work education was first established in Vietnam in 1957, in the southern part of the country. The early schools of social work were based on the French model, which focused on how to protect people against societal risks. It advocated that government had responsibility to protect its citizens from these risks. However, support for public social work education ceased following the Vietnam War. Although some private schools in the southern region of the country continued to provide social work training after the fall of the American-supported government in 1975, there was no public social work education offered for nearly three decades.

In 2004, however, public social work education was reintroduced when the Vietnamese government approved a social work syllabus. That year the Ministry of Education and Training granted permission for four schools of higher education to hold social work classes. The new social work education followed an American model, which emphasized using a person-centered, strengths-based perspective and "starting where the client is" to help people cope with the challenges of their social environments.

## UNIVERSITY OF HANOI SOCIAL WORK PROGRAM

The University of Hanoi (UH) was a large, highly respected university. Considered Vietnam's leading research and training center for the social sciences, it included the Colleges of Anthropology, Political Science, Psychology, Sociology, and several more. UH was one of the four schools approved to provide social work education.

To begin, UH's new social work program had twenty-one professors. However, few of them had any formal social work education or training, and most were from the UH Colleges of Anthropology and Sociology. In an effort to provide a more focused education, some adjunct professors who had worked in the field of social work before the Vietnam War were called out of retirement to teach a new generation of social workers.

Near the end of the social work program's first year, UH approved an expansion for the following year. In order to accommodate its growth, UH recruited additional professors to teach social work classes. Many of these were visiting professors from countries with a longer history with social work, including the United States and Australia. The second year of the social work program included classes and an introduction to fieldwork.

In their second year, students were to be assigned to field practicums in organizations that served vulnerable populations, but placement choices were limited. Social work practice had been largely absent from Vietnam for nearly thirty years, and social work was new to many people. Some were suspicious and thought social workers would try to change customs and norms. Given the novelty of the program and their lack of familiarity with the needs of social work students, few organizations would accept them in a practicum, and of those that would, only a few could provide the students with opportunities to observe social work practice in action. In addition, the students were encouraged to participate in field placements within close proximity of the university. As a result, there were far more students than available placements. Most placements hosted three or more students, and some had as many as ten students.

Many students in the social work program were interested in working with children, and some of them participated in field placements at the nearby Child Save orphanage, one of the few organizations that accepted social work students.

## CHILD SAVE

Founded in 1947, Child Save International was a global association of orphanages. It supported the operation of numerous orphanages and children's homes throughout the world and provided housing, medical care, and schools for orphaned and abandoned children, as well as supporting children's homes in more than one hundred countries. Many of the children's homes supported by Child Save International were based in Asia and worked toward the mission of "providing loving homes for all children."

Following the Vietnam War, the association reached an agreement with the Vietnamese government to establish several orphanages and children's homes throughout Vietnam, including Child Save in Hanoi. The local organization had a large compound, separated from the outside world by a high iron fence that surrounded the entire property. There was only one way in and one way out, and visitors entered through the security checkpoint. A large sign on the gate labeled the home as an orphanage, but within the fence, it resembled a small neighborhood of newly constructed buildings. The large headquarters building in the center of the complex was where administrators and senior staff worked. Surrounding the headquarters, there were twelve houses along the streets of the complex.

## A FAMILY MODEL

Each house was established using a family model. Most of the children were young when they arrived and typically remained in the same house during their entire stay at the orphanage. Nearly all the children came from poor families. About 80 percent of the children at the orphanage had no parents, but the remaining 20 percent lived at the orphanage because their families had to work remotely or because they displayed behavioral issues.

Each two-story house had a kitchen, a big living room, separate bathrooms for boys and girls, and several bedrooms. The children shared bedrooms, with three or four children in each room. Every house had a garden in the center courtyard where the "family" would raise vegetables and grow flowers.

Each house included at least ten children. In an effort to further approximate family life, the orphanage made efforts to place children of different ages in each home. Younger children usually attended a school on campus, while children of high school age attended schools in the surrounding neighborhood. Each house had a full-time female staff member who lived with the children, known as the Mother.

### THE MOTHERS

The role of Mother was a demanding one, as she was responsible for helping the children become adults. The Mother supervised the welfare of the children and the tasks assigned to them. One Mother lived and worked in each house full-time with the exception of the Lunar New Year holiday, when many returned briefly to their home communities. Many Mothers did not have their own families, and most had been widowed or divorced. None were currently married, and none had birth children living at home. The women hired as Mothers were generally not well educated. They lacked social work training and were not well paid by conventional standards; however, jobs were often scarce, and it was difficult for these women to find other positions outside of the orphanage.

### MAI LE, THE STUDENT

Mai Le was a vibrant young woman in her midtwenties. The older of two children, she lived with her family on the outskirts of Hanoi. Her parents owned a small bookstore and worked together to create a successful business. Like many Vietnamese parents, they believed that a child could survive in society only if they had a college degree and that society looked down on people who did not have formal education. As a result, they encouraged Mai to continue her education after high school.

One day a family friend who taught at UH asked Mai about her future after high school. "What are your plans once you graduate?" he asked.

"Well, I enjoy psychology and I am interested in research," Mai responded. "I'm just not really sure what to do at this point."

"Perhaps I can help you," he offered. "The University of Hanoi recently received approval for an undergraduate social work program. Social work just might be a good fit with your personality and interests."

"What is social work?" Mai asked.

"Well," the professor explained, "social work is a helping profession, and individual professionals are called social workers. Social workers engage people in their environments to address life challenges and enhance well-being. For example, social workers may have jobs involving child welfare, mental health, disabilities, or community development."

"That sounds interesting to me," Mai responded. *Okay, I'll just do that*, she decided. *All I need is a degree.*

"And, later," he continued, "if you decide you do not like the program, you can take an entrance exam for another program. I'm sure it will please your parents."

Although Mai was not familiar with social work, she decided it would give her a chance to learn and, more importantly, it would make her parents happy. It would also allow her another year to decide what work she wanted to do.

Mai applied to the social work program and was accepted into the inaugural cohort of seventy-five students. Every student followed the same schedule and attended classes together. "We got to know each other very well. We saw each other every day!" Mai explained. "After my first year of study was completed, the family friend who had encouraged me to apply asked me if I was planning to stay. He seemed surprised when I told him I enjoyed the program."

During the summer between her first and second years of the program, Mai volunteered at a children's summer camp in Hanoi. "I loved it. It was kind of like a practice course," she recalled. "I visited a lot of the slums and other poor areas of the city. There were many different people from many different places at the camp. A lot of the instructors were Australian, and some were American. They taught us more about the National Association of Social Workers [NASW] values of social work and practice in communities. The experience at the summer camp helped show me that I loved social work. I really wanted to stay with it."

## FIELD EXPERIENCES

Mai began field studies during her second year of the social work program. Due to her interest in child welfare, she was assigned to Child

Save. She spent time in different houses at the village and learned a great deal about the organizational structure of the orphanage. But she was often conflicted about the placement and her role there. Some of the Mothers assigned her to mop the floor or clean. "But I thought I was there to be with the children," Mai explained, "to understand the children better.

More concerning, however, were times when the children did not behave. Many of the older children, especially the boys, would cut school or try to run away. When this happened, the Mothers would often use corporal punishment to correct and control them. It sometimes seemed abusive. As Mai recalled, "My own family would use corporal punishment with my sister and me, but it was a rare thing. I know it is a common way to discipline children, but it is not right. The things I had learned, the social work values, seemed to conflict with this kind of treatment of children . . . but I felt like I could not say anything. If I said anything, I would damage the relationship between the orphanage and the school."

Nevertheless, one day Mai decided to discuss her feelings with Professor Anderson, one of the visiting American professors.

"Professor Anderson," she began, "I have been having some conflicting thoughts about my field placement. I would like your perspective on something. It really bothers me that the Mothers sometimes hit the children. It is very unethical."

Professor Anderson sat silently for a few seconds and then asked, "Mai, could you tell me more about why this troubles you so much?"

"Well," Mai shared, "I know that it is accepted for adults to slap or hit children. It is a common thing here in Vietnam. We have all grown up with it. My own parents would slap me when I misbehaved. I had teachers who would slap me and the other children when we made mistakes."

"So are you saying that corporal punishment is common in Vietnam?" the professor asked.

"Yes," Mai replied, "but there are problems in Vietnam today. I hear a lot about abuse. In class, we learned that we should remove this kind of punishment from our culture. Just the other day there was a story on television about a teacher who had done great harm to a student. It is the way we raise our children. Parents ask teachers to be strict with their children."

"Mai," Professor Anderson said, leaning toward her, "I hear you saying that corporal punishment is a common thing in Vietnamese culture. You said it was expected. You also said it was unethical. I'm wondering if you could tell me a little more about why you feel this way."

"Well, it is just hard to know when it is too much," Mai continued. "In class, the professors say such punishment is wrong."

The professor looked at her and said gently, "Mai, we also teach that it is important to try to understand what the other person is experiencing. Empathy and the ability to 'start where the client is' are essential parts of social work practice. People do not always do what we might believe is the right thing. In social work practice, it is important to try to walk in the shoes of the other person, to ask them about their world, to try to understand their perspective. There is always another story."

## MAI LE, THE FACULTY ASSISTANT

Following her graduation from the BSW program, Mai and two other members of her cohort were recruited to join the social work program as faculty assistants because they had performed so well and the school needed additional instructors. During that year, Mai taught assigned classes, recruited field placements, and served as a field liaison with students participating in field studies.

With the expansion of the program, it was challenging to find field placements for social work students. Mai and her fellow field liaisons worked hard to develop and maintain relationships with organizations willing to take on field students. Because of Mai's experiences at Child Save, she had reservations about the organization as a learning environment for social work students. "The people who supervise the students are not professionals," she confided to her coworkers. "They do not have social work education or skills . . ."

"Yes," another field liaison responded, "but they are willing to take our students, and we don't have many options."

As a field liaison, Mai wanted to help her students work through issues in their internships. She found that her students experienced some of the same anxieties she had experienced as a student, especially those regarding child welfare. Mai and the other field liaisons often met to discuss the field program and their students' progress.

Mai met with her students several times, especially during their second year of studies. Sometimes she met with them individually, but she usually met with them in groups. The students occasionally complained about their field placements, especially at the orphanage. One day they began to complain that they were assigned housework duties in the houses.

"Professor Le," Quy Tran began, "we do not feel we are learning what we are supposed to be learning. When we are at the orphanage, the Mothers treat us like staff. We are often assigned to wash dishes or mop floors."

"We cannot disagree with the Mother," Ha Lê added. "We are not to intervene between the Mother and a child. The Mothers want us to only observe. What do we learn by watching them hurt the children?"

"The other day," Quy said, "an older child was beaten with a cane when he had skipped school. We could only stand by and watch as the Mother hit the child over and over again."

Other students nodded.

"Some children are slapped when they make mistakes or perform badly at school," Cong Hoang said. "They become very upset."

As Mai looked around the room, she noticed that several students were tearful as they related things they had observed at the orphanage.

"What should we do when we see these things?" Cong asked. "We don't know what to do."

Later that day Mai reported this discussion to her fellow field liaisons. "This was a very bad time for me," Mai said. "The students witnessed the Mothers disciplining the children. Some of the things the students related sounded abusive."

"What did you say?" asked Linh Nguyen, one of the field liaisons.

"The students wanted me to tell them what to do," Mai responded. "They wanted me to give them answers. I did not know what to tell them."

"What *can* we tell them?" Linh asked.

"I remember how hard it was to do the field work," Mai continued. "It was hard to feel as though you had to keep the social work values to yourself when you were in the field. It was hard to be in a position where, as a student, you knew what was right and ethical. I knew what I had learned about the way children should be treated. I learned about the NASW Code of Ethics, and I knew that I should apply these ethical principles to my work. It was hard to do that during field placements. As a student, I felt like I had no power to say anything, even when I knew something was wrong. I remember that, and now my students are experiencing that same anxiety. I want to be available to and supportive of our students."

A few days later Mai revisited the subject of abuse with her fellow field liaisons. "As you know, some of my field students spoke about the level of corporal punishment used at the orphanage. We are Vietnamese. We understand our culture . . . but the things we teach our students sometimes conflict with the way our culture sees child welfare and child discipline.

"It can be very distressing," Linh replied. "It was hard to understand when I was a student. I am sure it is hard for our students as well."

"Yes," Mai answered, "but we are responsible for helping students learn how to apply social work education to real-world problems. Corporal punishment is not in line with social work values."

"But, Mai," Linh reminded, "we must maintain positive relationships with the few organizations who accept our students. If we fail to maintain a positive relationship with the Mothers, we may lose the opportunity for our students to learn from field placements at all."

*How do we balance the needs of the university, the needs of the students, and the needs of the organizations?* Mai wondered.

Mai continued to ponder ways she could address the concerns of her students and finally decided to contact the orphanage to request a meeting with the Head Mother. Mai made several phone calls before she was able to speak with the woman who was senior to all other Mothers at Child Save. They made an appointment to meet the next day. Mai spent the remainder of the afternoon compiling the concerns of her students and reviewing the field office's agreement with Child Save and the NASW Code of Ethics. As she prepared, Mai felt some anxiety about the meeting. *I hope I can make the Head Mother understand the way children should be treated.*

## MEETING WITH THE HEAD MOTHER

The next day Mai made her way to the Child Save, arriving at the orphanage fifteen minutes before her appointment. The guard at the entrance gate recognized her from her own field placement two years before. He provided her with directions to the house where the Head Mother lived. *I remember when I was a student here*, Mai thought as she walked through the streets of the village. *Even then I questioned the ways the Mothers disciplined the children.*

Mai knocked on the door, and a small woman welcomed her. She was less than five feet tall and very slight of frame, and she appeared to be about fifty years of age.

"When we spoke yesterday," the Mother said to Mai, "you mentioned you were here as a social work student two years ago. I still don't remember you, but I talked with the Mother where you worked."

*What did she tell you?* Mai wondered nervously. *Did she mention that I thought she treated the children too roughly?* "Thank you for allowing me into your home," Mai said.

In response to Mai's questions, the Mother explained that she was a widow with adult children. She began working at the orphanage after her own children had left home and after completing two years of business school. After five years at the orphanage, she was recently promoted to supervisor because of her education and work experience.

While they got acquainted, Mai noticed the house was tidy but busy. Two small children were playing in the living room, and the smell of pho was in the air. Mai could hear the sounds of the clothes washer.

"Mother," Mai began, "I wanted to meet with you because my students have some concerns." Mai waited for the Mother to reply, but she remained silent, so Mai continued. "The students feel that some of the children are treated in a rough manner. One of my students has reported a child being beaten with a cane." Mai removed a copy of the NASW Code of Ethics from her satchel and handed it to the Mother. "We use this at the university to help guide our students."

The Mother looked at the booklet and placed it on the table. "And you, Mai, what do you feel about these things the students have told you?" she asked. "What does your book tell you?"

"I don't know the situation directly," Mai responded. *I need to be respectful*, she thought. *I need to maintain a good relationship with this woman. We have so few places the students can learn. The orphanage is one of the only field placements we have!* "However, when I was a student here, I saw Mothers being severe, at times, to the children. They would sometimes pull the hair of the children or slap them very hard. This is not ethical. It is not correct. It is not what we are teaching in social work education."

"Does your social work education teach you to come into the home of another person and decide for them what is right and what is wrong?" the Mother asked. "Your students are here for a few hours, for a few weeks. The Mothers are with the children every day, all day. Your students do not know the children. They do not know the dangers these children face. They do not know how hard the Mothers work to keep these children from harm all day, every day."

Mai raised her hand to interrupt, but the Mother continued. "For instance, the boy who was caned has a very severe behavioral issue. He makes choices that put him and the other children in danger. How do you expect the Mother to control him and the other nine children in the home if she cannot command respect? The children who are slapped are disrespectful. You yourself know the danger to children who are disrespectful. Do you not agree that it is important to teach children how to conduct themselves in a way that helps them get on in the world?"

Mai nodded in agreement, and the Mother continued. "The children here are broken. They do not always respond to softness. And all of the Mothers here work very, very hard. They are here every day and have almost no relief for themselves. If they are sick, they must take care of the children. If they are tired, they must take care of the children. They work very hard and get very little respect." With this, the Mother rose and straightened her spine, saying "I will not allow your students to be disrespectful to these women who work so hard and are the only ones who really take care of these children. You have training, but you do not work here. Your books cannot tell people what is best. What is best is what is best at the time."

"Mother, I hear what you are saying. Please understand that my role is to help the students grow in their knowledge. I am very grateful that you allow them here so that they may learn from you, but . . ."

The Mother raised her hand to silence Mai. "Your students are children themselves. You should ask your students to walk in the shoes of the Mother before they make pronouncements."

With these words, Mai remembered Professor Anderson's advice. "Mother, thank you so much for taking the time to speak with me."

As Mai walked back through the streets of the orphanage, she reflected on the conversation and remembered how Professor Anderson had encouraged her to put herself in the place of the other person. *We are experts*, Mai acknowledged to herself, *but maybe the real experts are the people who do the work, the people who do the work directly. It is important to learn things, but maybe social work students can learn the most about children from the people who are with the children. What do I tell my students?*

## MEETING WITH THE STUDENTS

The following day, as her next meeting with the field students drew near, Mai wondered what she could say. She knew they were frustrated and eager to make change. They would ask if she had told the Head Mother what was right, if she had been able to correct the Head Mother's thinking.

The field students had gathered in the conference room. As she walked down the hall, Mai could hear them talking and whispering to one another. She took a deep breath and entered the room.

# 13

# BREWS AND FIELD INSTRUCTOR BLUES (A)

*Linda Ayscue Gupta and Abigail D. Kinnebrew*

Five weeks after a remediation plan was put in place that required Anthony Woods to complete all field hours on-site at his field agency, his off-site field instructor, Phillip Thompson, went to meet him there. Phillip arrived a few minutes before their scheduled one P.M. supervision session. Anthony was not there, and an administrative staff member said he had left that morning to go to work at the coffee shop. Phillip assumed he was coming back because they had confirmed the meeting the day before by email. But after waiting twenty minutes, Phillip called Anthony's cell phone. "Hey, Anthony, where are you?"

"I'm at a coffee shop," Anthony replied.

"We have supervision," Phillip reminded.

---

This decision case was prepared solely to provide material for class discussion and not to suggest either effective or ineffective handling of the situation depicted. While based on field research regarding an actual situation, names and certain facts may have been disguised to protect confidentiality. The authors wish to thank the case reporter for cooperation in making this account available for the benefit of social work students and practitioners.

"Oh, I'm sorry! I totally forgot."

"Rather than you coming here, since you have transportation issues, I can come to you."

"Um . . . are you sure?"

"Yes."

"Um . . . okay."

"What coffee shop?" Phillip asked.

"I'm at GrillMarx downtown."

*That doesn't sound like a coffee shop*, Phillip thought, as he headed out the door. *Maybe it's a panini place. But according to the remediation plan, he's supposed to be at the agency "during all field hours"!*

## UNITED WAY OF WEST ALABAMA

United Way of West Alabama was a leader in fund-raising for a number of community service partner agencies in Tuscaloosa. Originally founded as Community Chest of Tuscaloosa in 1946, it had expanded to serve residents of the city and nine surrounding counties. The agency occupied a suite in a large office building that housed other service and health care providers and that was located on a city street a couple of miles from the University of Alabama campus. It provided leadership for local community nonprofits in forming coalitions and building community resources in the areas of health, education, and income stability through fund-raising and grant making. It also provided information and referral services to individuals to link them to appropriate resources. A staff of eleven was headed by President and CEO Rick Watson, MPH.

## RICK WATSON, UNITED WAY PRESIDENT AND CEO

Rick Watson was a white man in his early forties with a beard and medium-length, wavy brown hair. He typically wore khaki pants and polo shirts. He had served as a task supervisor to social work students from the University of Alabama School of Social Work for the past five years, three of which were while he was at the United Way of West Alabama. Those he worked with at the university described him as easy-going and affable but also very serious, passionate, and enthusiastic about his work. Rick was recruited to be a task supervisor by faculty members who had previously collaborated with him on projects while he was working at another nonprofit organization. In his current position, he managed a thirty-member board of directors and a staff of eleven and oversaw the programming of the agency and the work of approximately eight hundred volunteers. During the legislative session, he also did a great deal of lobbying at the state capital in Montgomery, which took him away from the office quite a bit.

As a task supervisor, Rick was engaged with his students and was very good at giving them specific learning tasks appropriate for their level of knowledge and skills. He did have some difficulty at times keeping up with reviewing and providing feedback on process recordings due to his many responsibilities.

## UNIVERSITY OF ALABAMA SCHOOL OF SOCIAL WORK

The University of Alabama School of Social Work provided field education to more than six hundred students in MSW and BSW programs each year. More specifically, students in their MSW foundation year completed 450 hours of field placement along with an accompanying field seminar class. These hours were spread out evenly across the semester at the rate of sixteen to eighteen hours per week. However, before spring semester classes, students completed a "block week," in which they spent forty hours in their field placements.

## SUSAN DIBLER, DIRECTOR OF FIELD EDUCATION

Dr. Susan Dibler was the director of field education in the School of Social Work. She was a white woman in her early fifties with medium-length, straight, blonde hair and an inviting smile. She oversaw the placements of all MSW/BSW students in their field internships, the implementation of field seminar classes, and the training and supervision of the field instructors and field liaisons, as well as serving on all relevant School of Social Work committees as a faculty member. She would also become directly involved in situations when the university was considering removing and/or failing a student in field placement. Susan herself served as a field liaison for ten to fifteen students who had off-site supervisors or were in placements that diverged from the standard model of field education.

## PHILLIP THOMPSON, FIELD INSTRUCTOR

Phillip Thompson, a thirty-eight-year-old white man with graying blond hair and a stocky build, was a PhD candidate in social work at the University of Alabama. Originally from Britain, he had been in the United States for fourteen years and was married to an American. He was a licensed social worker who had a BA in theology from Queen's University of Belfast and an MSW from San Diego State University. He had worked for six years as a program manager in an adolescent group home prior to earning his MSW and for an additional two and a half years post-MSW in adolescent mental health and recovery.

Phillip's research interests were positive youth development and substance use. As a PhD candidate, he had an office on campus and provided field instruction to a group of students and helped with observing and assessing students in the implementation of Screening, Brief Intervention, and Referral to Treatment (SBIRT), a supplemental requirement of all foundation-level MSW students.

Phillip was in his first year of providing field instruction for students and took his field instructor role very seriously.

## ANTHONY WOODS, GRADUATE STUDENT INTERN

Anthony Woods was a twenty-five-year-old white social work student intern at United Way of Western Alabama. He was of average height and thin, with glasses and long, mousy brown hair that he wore in a ponytail. He wore khakis and polos and often sported a fashion baseball cap. Phillip described him as mellow and reflective but sometimes a little cocky and sarcastic.

Anthony had a BA in sociology with a minor in child advocacy from Auburn University. He had a clear vision of what he wanted to do with his MSW degree: work in mental health with adolescent males.

Anthony was admitted late to the MSW program. He had just graduated from his undergraduate program during the summer and moved from a more rural part of the state shortly before the beginning of classes. Despite this, he started the placement on time and, by all reports, did well. He was assigned to United Way of Western Alabama under the task supervision of Rick Watson, and Phillip Thompson was his field instructor.

In this field placement, Anthony's main responsibilities were assisting with event planning and staffing for fund-raising events, assisting with volunteer coordination, and gathering information from partner agencies and literature searches for grant applications. He received task supervision from Rick on a regular basis. On alternate weeks, Anthony also met with Phillip at the agency for one hour of supervision focused on Anthony's learning and progress in field. In addition, Anthony often dropped by Phillip's office to check in when he was on campus or called Phillip on the phone between supervision sessions. Phillip believed they had established a good supervisory relationship.

Phillip observed that Anthony's group of friends in the MSW program consisted of mostly conservative, middle-class white men. One regularly wore an NRA cap to school that Phillip thought seemed to "give other students the middle finger." By late October, Phillip sensed that Anthony was struggling with the material in his course on diversity and difference, particularly with reconciling his perceived privilege as a white male in the social work profession. Phillip arranged for Anthony to meet him for supervision on campus.

"As a white male, it can be uncomfortable at times," Phillip offered and paused. *It's important that I give you room to sit with that.*

"Yeah, in diversity class, all the problems in the world are tied to us," Anthony responded. "Sometimes I don't know what to say or how to say it."

"Stay with that tension, Anthony—that discomfort," Phillip invited. "What does it bring up for you?"

"Well, everybody acts like if you're a white male, your life is a breeze. It ain't been no piece of cake for me and my family, man."

"Do you want to say more about that?" Phillip waited patiently.

Anthony sat quietly for a few moments, sighed, and then began. "Look, my dad's people were all farmers. It got harder and harder to make a living. When I was about fourteen, he went looking for one of those good-paying jobs on an oil rig. He got one, but he was gone six months at a time. When he came back, he was drinkin' hard. Mama was on his case real bad. 'Damned if you do, and damned if you don't,' Daddy used to say. 'Ain't no pleasing her.' "

"Sounds like you were close to your dad if he was confiding in you," Phillip responded.

"Yeah, I was. Nobody's perfect. He was tryin' hard to put food on the table and make a better life for us. Sometimes he'd let me go with him when he met up with his friends. Everybody loved him. Once in a while he'd let me take a drink with them. When he went back on the rig, one of his friends would slip me some beer from time to time. Then Mama found out and threw me out of the house. 'You are not going to be a drunkard and live under my roof!' It went downhill from there."

*That's a pretty strong response*, Phillip thought. "Did you see that coming?"

"Not at the time, but a lot of stuff was going on. My grades had slid. I was going to school when I felt like it. I was gettin' into arguments with her and my sister all the time. I won't bore you with all the details, but it took me a few years to get myself straight." Anthony paused and then added, "I spent some time homeless, ended up in foster care for a year, and did some other things I don't want to remember.

"Where was your dad in all this?" Phillip explored.

"Off." Anthony paused. "He was working on the rig while he could. He still needed to take care of my mom and my sister. He 'couldn't do nothing with me,' he said when the social worker asked him about a plan for me."

*So how did you get from there to here?* Phillip wondered. "Anthony, what do you think about your progress? You graduated college last year. Now you are in graduate school.

"It's been a long road. When I was in foster care, I got diagnosed with attention deficit disorder [ADD]. That explained a lot about why I felt so stressed all the time. The older I got, the more things I had to organize."

*Man, I know how that feels.* Phillip wandered off into his own thoughts. *When I was diagnosed with ADD, I was upset and relieved at the same time. I wonder if he has learned how to cope with it.*

"I stopped drinking while I was on the meds." Anthony's voice interrupted his thoughts. "I started doing better in school. Mom let me come back home. I graduated community college and then went to Auburn. I was doing good until I joined the fraternity." Anthony faltered and then plunged ahead. "You know how it is. Sometimes we did some partying, and one night we got a wild hair and decided to do some racing. It was the middle of the night. Nobody was on the road, so we thought we were good."

"But you weren't?" Phillip asked.

"Nope," Anthony confirmed. "Flashing lights, sirens, cold handcuffs around my wrists. Nobody was hurt, thank God, but it was a wake-up call. I'm back in recovery now."

"So that's it," Phillip surmised, "the reason you weren't able to be placed in a micro setting this year?"

"Yep, you know I eventually want to work in a mental health setting with adolescent males," Anthony offered. "I've pretty much ruined my chances of that unless I can convince a recovery setting to take me on as an intern next year."

"Anthony, that's real. Thanks for sharing that with me." Phillip continued, "It really helps me understand some of the challenges you have faced, and now I think I understand why you were triggered by the talk of 'white male privilege.' "

"You got it." With a sarcastic grin, Anthony mocked, "I don't feel 'privileged,' never felt 'privileged.' Always had to scrap for everything I got, though I admit sometimes I've been my own worst enemy."

*I know I'm taking a risk here, but I think he's up to it.* Phillip ventured, "So let's use this. What can you glean from your own experience that can help you with your clients, especially those who, like you, haven't all been able to start at the gate?"

"What do you mean?" Anthony sat forward in his chair. "Oh, I get it!" He was very still. "So I didn't start at the gate because we were poor, because my father drank too much, because he was gone, because I had ADD, because I now have a substance use disorder. And others don't start at the gate because they are female or African American or transgender, and others have put up barriers for them. They have been invisible to me. I didn't see their pain because I didn't live it. I'm a barrier myself. Man, that's really sad."

"Yes, it is," Phillip said, speaking softly now, "but not as sad as not recognizing that at all."

"So it's not whose pain is the worst, but I need to hear their pain." Anthony paused and then added, "Like you just heard my pain."

"Exactly," Phillip said. "That's what we mean by 'use of self.' It's part of our professional identity as social workers to be able to recognize, respect, empathize, and respond to the pain of others.

As he stood up to leave, Anthony offered Phillip a handshake. "Thanks for helping me with this, Phillip. I have overcome a lot and I'm still pluggin'. I'm still learning and that's okay. For the first time, I think I'm finally getting this 'diversity and difference' stuff."

*He's going to be okay*, Phillip thought as he watched Anthony head out the door. For the next several weeks, he was right.

## FALL SEMESTER: THE FINAL LIAISON MEETING

At the final liaison meeting of the fall semester, Phillip and Anthony met with Rick to review Anthony's performance.

"Overall, Anthony's doing well," Rick summarized, "but he has some trouble with organization, punctuality, and time management."

"Yes," Phillip agreed. "Anthony has owned some challenges keeping up with hours, coming in on time, and meeting deadlines."

"Well," Rick said as he fixed his gaze on Anthony, "I've trusted him with the freedom to set his own schedule and work off-site if appropriate because that's what macro practitioners need to do." Anthony shuffled in his seat and looked down.

*I'm not completely sure that's a good idea*, Phillip mused. But out loud he said, "Rick, tell us exactly what you need from Anthony going forward. I'll take notes."

Still not taking his eyes off Anthony, Rick responded, "During spring semester, I'm going to be out of the office a lot, lobbying in Montgomery. I need you to be more of a self-starter. I need you to be more organized. 9:00 A.M. is 9:00 A.M.; it's not 10:30. And close of business does not mean 8:57 P.M."

"Look, I'm confused. You told me to set my own schedule," Anthony argued. "I did that."

"You know, Anthony, if you make a 9:00 A.M. appointment with an agency director to gather information for a grant, then you show up at 9:00 A.M., not at 10:30. Same thing with phone conferences," Rick insisted.

"You know I called him later to apologize and let him know why I was . . ."

"After I told you to do that," Rick interrupted. "I need you to be where you are supposed to be, call when you are supposed to call, finish a task at the time you say you are going to finish it. It's important that we, as an agency, are dependable. Is that clear?"

"We already talked about this, and I told you I would do this." Anthony was irritated.

"Rick, Anthony and I talked about some strategies to help with prioritizing and accomplishing time-sensitive tasks," Phillip offered. "Is there any additional information you want to offer here?"

Softening a bit, Rick explained, "So when Anthony completes a task, it is usually done well. But I have to start him, monitor his work, and sometimes push him to finish it." Looking at Anthony again, he continued, "We've already talked about this. I don't want to beat a dead horse, but I'm not going to have time second semester to hold your hand. I need you to set submission dates that will give me time to comment on your work. I need you to come to weekly meetings with me with questions or problems you might be having. I don't want to find out about these a couple of days before the information is due. I don't want a repeat of what happened on the last project."

"What happened?" Phillip was puzzled.

"Do you want to tell him or do I?" Rick waited for Anthony.

"I gave him some information too late," Anthony admitted.

"Specifically?" Rick prompted.

"I gave him information on our last fund-raiser on Friday night," Anthony mumbled, clearly embarrassed.

Rick spoke to Phillip. "I said close of business Thursday, as I had planned to work on the report Friday for our board meeting Monday night. As it turns out, I had to complete it over the weekend. Like I said, I don't want to beat a dead horse. I just want to be clear about what is going well and help Anthony make the changes he needs to make to be successful."

Addressing both Rick and Anthony, Phillip offered, "It seems like you've been clear about what you need, Rick. And, Anthony, I appreciate that you brought this up to me on your own and asked for help. Is there anything else I can do to assist?"

"We've got this now, don't you think?" Rick turned to Anthony who, looking relieved, gave him a thumbs up.

Phillip remained mildly concerned. *I know Anthony has a lot going on. More is going to be expected of him in the coming semester, and he is going to have to take more responsibility for his schedule, his work, and his learning. Yeah, he's making it now*, Phillip thought, *but I am afraid this could be the straw that breaks the camel's back.*

At their next supervision session, Phillip followed up with Anthony to express his concerns. Being the most direct he had ever been, Phillip said, "It's really, really imperative that you are on it."

"I know, Phillip," Anthony responded, appearing confused. "Why are we talking about this again? I don't know what else I can say."

"Listen, Anthony, you know when we met in my office and you told me about being diagnosed with ADD? Well, I didn't tell you at that time that I also have a diagnosis of ADD. And I can tell you that from my personal and professional experience, this type of arrangement, as it pertains to task supervision, might not be enough structure for you. In my career, this has been hard at times. It has been a real growing edge for me." Then Phillip added, "Deadlines are going to be looser, but there is more onus on you to deliver the products. Your role here is to complete the research tasks you are given."

"Yeah, yeah," Anthony replied. "I understand."

*I hope you heard me*, Phillip thought. *That wasn't the enthusiastic response I hoped for.* "You're going to have to be organized," Phillip tried again, "as it pertains to time and dates." Phillip was earnest now. "You're going to have to structure yourself. If you need any help with that, any additional tips, will you contact me?"

"Phillip, I get it!" Anthony said.

Later, as he drove away, Phillip reassured himself, *Rick has a good sense of what's in Anthony's wheelhouse, and he said they've got it. These are good mezzo and macro opportunities for him.*

In January, Anthony called Phillip. "I'm really sick, man. I'm not going to make it to block week."

"Are you all right? What's wrong?" Phillip was genuinely concerned.

"I've been sick all Christmas. First, I thought it was just a cold; then I got a sore throat and started running a fever. I had a really bad cough and I couldn't shake it. I didn't want to go to the doctor; my funds are low this month. Finally, my Mom put her foot down and made me go to urgent care. She had to pay the bill. I had walking pneumonia! They put me on a ton of medicine. I'm slowly getting better, but I'm not back in Tuscaloosa yet.

"I'm sorry to hear that but glad to hear you're on the mend. Listen, Anthony, it's a big deal to miss the whole block week. You will have to make up any missed hours, so get back as soon as you can. And make sure you let Rick know about this. Also, be forewarned that you might need to get a doctor's note saying you should be excused from school for X number of days."

"No problem," Anthony responded. "I already emailed Rick."

During the second week of field placement, Anthony emailed Phillip that he had made it into the office on Thursday of the block week for a few hours.

The third week Phillip visited the agency for supervision. When he arrived, Rick called him into his office. "Look, I know Anthony was sick block week, but since he's been back, he's already been late two days and left early two days. I've got him tracking some legislation and doing some lit searches for a grant we might submit. I need you to communicate with Anthony that he needs to make these deadlines and show up. We can't start this up again."

"Sure, I'll talk to him," Phillip agreed.

When Phillip mentioned Rick's concerns, Anthony responded, "Look, I was sick for three weeks and had been back for two full days before I started to come late and leave early." Phillip noted that he seemed apologetic and uncomfortable.

"So what's this about, Anthony? If you've been released by your doctor to come back to school, why are you coming late and leaving early?" *I'm just about over this*, Phillip thought.

"I lost my ride, man." Anthony threw his hands up and let them drop helplessly in his lap.

"So how will you solve this?" Phillip asked, to elicit solutions. Fifteen minutes later Anthony had developed a plan to take the free campus connector and walk the remainder of the way. Alternatively, if the weather was bad, he would walk three blocks and catch the city bus for the remainder of the journey to the agency.

"I didn't know where to start," Anthony admitted. "I never took a city bus before."

Two weeks later Phillip went back to the agency. Rick was exuberant. "Whatever you did worked! Anthony's been here on time, every day, all day!"

"And turning in work on time?" Phillip asked.

"So far, so good!" Rick cheered.

In his meeting with Anthony, Phillip asked, "How's your transportation plan working?"

"Great," Anthony replied. "The best part of it is I don't have to be dependent on anybody else. I'm in control; that's a huge relief."

*So much time lost, so much stress for something so simple*—Phillip felt a twinge of sadness—*all because he was embarrassed to ask for help, to say what he didn't know.* He continued, "Ready for the next challenge?"

Anthony nodded.

"You're doing great, according to both you and Rick. But you're kind of in a hole here with the time you missed block week. Maybe you can make up some time on Fridays." The two of them spent the next thirty minutes calendaring the time through the remainder of the semester, and Anthony submitted it to Rick for his approval.

During their next session, Phillip combined supervision with the SBIRT observation that was part of the MSW foundation-year requirements. Anthony admitted, "I am so nervous; I haven't had a lot of time with clients."

"I know, Anthony," Phillip said reassuringly, "but I think you will do fine."

Anthony did not perform to passing standards. *It was terrible*, Phillip admitted to himself. He told Anthony, "You'll need to come back to do it again." Phillip couldn't bring himself to tell Anthony he "failed."

That night Phillip received an email from Anthony:

> Phillip, I am really worried. I wasn't fully honest in supervision. Rick is really pissed off at me. I have not been doing the work I am supposed to be doing. I have not been coming in this last couple of weeks. Rick wants us all to have a meeting next week. I am trying to figure out what to do about this. I am really worried. Please help me with this.

*What the heck?* Phillip thought. *I can't believe this! He was doing so well! No calls from him; no calls from Rick. No wonder he failed the SBIRT observation.*

Phillip picked up the phone to call Anthony. After multiple rings, he heard "You have reached Anthony Woods. Please leave a message . . ."

"Hey, Anthony, this is Phillip. Give me a call so we can plan to meet."

*Okay*, Phillip thought, *maybe he'll see an email first*. He wrote:

> Anthony, I got your email and tried to call you right away but just got your voice mail. Would it be possible for us to meet on campus tomorrow at 9 AM? If that is not good, I will be free again at 1 PM. Please call me back as soon as possible to confirm one of these times or to set a time to speak by phone.

Five days later Anthony responded via text: "Sorry. I was out of cell phone range. I was on a hiking trip on the Appalachian Trail."

Phillip texted back: "We have a meeting set with Rick at the usual time on Wednesday. I will meet with you first, and the two of us will then meet with Rick." He sent the same message via email.

When Phillip went to meet with Anthony and Rick on Wednesday, Rick intercepted him. "Hey, Phillip, Anthony has not been in, he has not done his work, and I had to hire a temp this week to catch up on the work!"

"Rick, why didn't you call me when this started again?" he asked.

"I was in Montgomery. I didn't realize he was so far behind. I can't babysit him anymore." Rick turned on his heel to go back down the hall.

"Rick," Phillip asked, "what are you telling me?"

"I'm done with him!" Rick said. "You and Susan deal with this."

Then Phillip went to talk with Anthony. "Anthony, I need to get some facts from you first before we meet with Rick.

"Rick is a hypocrite!" Anthony said.

Taken aback, Phillip responded, "Before we go there, help me with this timeline. I saw you last Wednesday for the observation. I had seen you and Rick just two weeks before. At that time, both of you told me you were pleased with your work. You were coming in on time, meeting deadlines, fulfilling all your hours. In fact, we calendared your makeup hours through the rest of the semester."

Anthony nodded in agreement.

"But," Phillip continued, "your email last week said that you had not been 'fully honest' with me, that you had stopped coming in regularly the last couple of weeks, stopped doing your work."

Anthony again nodded his assent.

"Am I understanding this correctly then—that almost as soon as you were successful and even planned for your continued success, you . . . "

"Sabotaged myself," Anthony interrupted.

"Sounds like that's not a new concept for you." Phillip cleared his throat. "Anyway, I'm glad you recognize that pattern, but we have a major problem here. Did you come in on time today?"

"Yes, I did. I was here at nine A.M. sharp. I thought I should make a fresh start," Anthony offered, "but Rick read me the riot act. That's what I'm trying to tell you. He's a hypocrite. He is not here. He shows up when he wants to. He leaves when he wants to. He doesn't answer my emails."

Phillip said, "Can we discuss this with Rick?"

"No," Anthony responded indignantly. "I am done with him. He is a fucking hypocrite!"

"That is not appropriate, Anthony," Phillip said, wincing. "You are not Rick. You do not know what he is doing. He is the director of the agency. I don't think it's helpful to compare yourself to him."

Anthony glowered silently.

"So what's the plan now, Anthony?" Phillip asked. "Did you and Rick talk about that?"

"He told me he hired a temp. She's done all my work," Anthony grumbled. "Now I don't have anything to do!"

"Anthony, the bottom line is this: you've got to demonstrate that you can do the work and that's not happening. Think about that and let me know if/when you are ready to meet with Rick."

Phillip walked back into Rick's office and said, "So I hear that you are done with him. I want to go back to talk to Susan about this. Is there anything else I should know?"

"I'm not sure what he's doing," Rick said. "I suspect that he's drinking at night."

"Drinking!" *Oh, no!* Phillip thought, *I've been putting all of this down to his ADD.* "Are you sure?"

"Of course, I can't be sure!" Rick exclaimed. "I just know he's late in the morning. He's tired all the time. He's disheveled."

*What if Anthony has relapsed?* Phillip wondered as he drove to Susan's office. *That would make sense . . . that would explain everything. Oh flip!* Phillip thought with a start, *Anthony has relapsed. He is using again.*

Seconds later Phillip slammed his hands on the steering wheel. *I don't have the skill to reconcile these two people. They are so shut off, so angry, and in different parts of the building. I have never seen Rick angry before. This is really over . . .*

At Susan's office, Phillip burst through her doorway.

"Are you okay?" Susan asked, startled.

Gasping for breath, Phillip replied, "Rick's fired Anthony."

"What? Why?" Susan asked.

"I think he's relapsed," Phillip explained. "He lied to everybody. Rick thinks he's drinking at night. He said he shows up—if he shows up—late, tired, and disheveled. All the work Anthony said he was doing . . . he has lied to everybody."

"You don't know that," Susan replied. "You're jumping to conclusions. You may be identifying with Anthony too much."

"Whatever, Susan, he's not doing the work," Phillip responded, frustrated. "When he's on it, he does a really good job. But then he's MIA, often with no warning. Every time I think we've made a breakthrough, he maintains about two weeks before he reverts back to his old ways. I don't know if he's using, derailed by his ADD, reenacting what he experienced with his father, whatever. The bottom line is that I'm not able to help him—or Rick. I've tried everything I know. And I don't want us to lose this placement for other students."

"Let's do this," Susan suggested. "I think I should meet with them immediately. I'll call them right now to make sure they're both still there and let them know I'm on my way. I want to try to smooth the situation over, both to salvage the relationship with the agency and to get Anthony and Rick in the same room to discuss the conflict.

"That's a good idea, Susan," Phillip agreed. "Maybe a visit from the field director will help Anthony realize how serious this is. He's about to fail field."

Susan called Rick while Phillip was still there and set up a meeting with Rick and Anthony that afternoon. Phillip left with a glimmer of hope that Susan could help them both get back on track.

The next morning Phillip dropped by Susan's office to find out what had transpired the day before.

"I went to the agency to meet with Rick and Anthony," Susan began. "Rick denied telling you that Anthony had relapsed. Anthony denied refusing to work with Rick, and Rick denied refusing to work with Anthony. I asked specifically if there was any issue with alcohol. Anthony said that he was in reduction. I resolved the situation and put a remediation plan in place, calendaring the rest of the year. As part of the plan, we required Anthony to be present at the agency for all field hours."

"I feel like an idiot," Phillip responded when Susan finished her account. "They probably thought I overreacted."

"Yeah, well, that's easy to do when everyone's so angry," Susan said reassuringly.

As they probed Phillip's response, he acknowledged, "I own that I care for Anthony professionally. I see his strengths. Maybe I do identify with him. I was afraid he had relapsed."

"Better that mistake than missing something altogether," Susan offered.

*At the same time*, Phillip thought, *you threw me under the bus. At some level, all of you threw me under the bus. I know what I heard. I feel like a rank amateur. This is embarrassing.*

"So," Phillip asked, gathering his thoughts, "what should I do next?"

At the next regularly scheduled supervision, Phillip checked in with Anthony about the situation. He reviewed the remediation plan with him.

"I can do it, Phillip," Anthony said optimistically. "I did it before and I can do it again."

*Been there, done that*, Phillip thought, but he kept his doubts to himself. "Anthony, I wish you had informed me of your concerns regarding Rick earlier. Sometimes you have to advocate for yourself with your task supervisor. This is a skill you will need in practice." They contracted to work on this in future supervision sessions, using role play to practice addressing his learning needs.

"Rick's given me new tasks now that I know I will be able to do. I'm back on track," Anthony said. And he was.

## THE PUB MEETING

In April, Phillip went to the agency to meet with Anthony at their agreed-on time, 1 P.M. No one, not even Anthony, was present at the agency. An administrative staff member returning from lunch told Phillip that Anthony had come in for about ten minutes in the morning but had left to go to work at the coffee shop. *The coffee shop?* Phillip was puzzled, but he waited. He assumed Anthony was coming back because they had confirmed the meeting the day before by email. *This is part of his endearing growing edge*, Phillip thought. But after waiting twenty minutes, Phillip called Anthony's cell phone. "Hey, Anthony, where are you?"

"I'm at a coffee shop," Anthony replied.

"We have supervision," Phillip reminded.

"Oh, I'm sorry! I totally forgot."

"Rather than you coming here, since you have transportation issues, I can come to you."

"Um . . . are you sure?"

"Yes."

"Um . . . okay."

"What coffee shop?" Phillip asked.

"I'm at GrillMarx downtown."

*That doesn't sound like a coffee shop*, Phillip thought as he headed out the door. *Maybe it's a panini place. But according to the remediation plan, he's supposed to be at the agency "during all field hours"!*

When Phillip arrived, he saw that it was an open-style burger and brew restaurant. He walked in to find Anthony sitting at the bar with his binder on one side and a pint of beer on the other.

*What?!* Phillip thought. *You invited me to meet you in a pub?! What were you thinking?*

# 14

## COLLATERAL DAMAGE (A)

*Betty L. Wilson and Terry A. Wolfer*

Amanda Byrnes, an undergraduate psychology student at Western Illinois University, decided to tell Heidi Donaldson that a field instructor had sexually harassed her and treated her unfairly. Heidi was the assistant director of the university's Office of Civil Rights and Diversity.

"Anything you say with us will be kept confidential unless you decide to pursue action," Heidi reassured her.

"What does that look like?" Amanda asked.

"We can move forward with this," Heidi explained, "only if you decide to go public, to attach your name."

---

This decision case was prepared solely to provide material for class discussion and not to suggest either effective or ineffective handling of the situation depicted. While based on field research regarding an actual situation, names and certain facts may have been disguised to protect confidentiality. The authors wish to thank the case reporter for cooperation in making this account available for the benefit of social work students and practitioners.

"So that means that he will know I'm the one who reported it?" Amanda's voice suddenly became quieter.

"Yes," Heidi said.

*Oh, gosh, I really can't do it now.* Amanda paused, her mind racing. *If it was anonymous, I wouldn't feel so bad. But having my name attached to it, everyone in the office is gonna know, even the guys. And he knows where I live! I can't move forward with this*—Amanda paused again—*but I can't walk away from it either.*

## WESTERN ILLINOIS UNIVERSITY

Western Illinois University (WIU) was a public university located in the rural town of Macomb. Founded in 1899 as the Western Illinois State Normal School, a small training college for teachers, it had expanded its curriculum and programs to offer a wide variety of degrees at the undergraduate, graduate, and doctoral levels. As a result, it consisted of five academic colleges: Arts and Sciences, Business and Technology, Education and Human Services, Fine Arts and Communication, and the Honors School of Extended Studies. Enrollment at the university was approximately nine thousand students.

## PSYCHOLOGY DEPARTMENT

Housed in Waggoner Hall, the Department of Psychology had more than four hundred undergraduate students and fifty graduate students. Many faculty members were active practitioners and well-published authors, and they held degrees from major universities across the country. Undergraduate students were encouraged to work closely with faculty on research projects and serve on department committees to help prepare them for graduate studies and future careers in the field. The department was equipped with laboratories and advanced video and audio equipment that students could use to conduct trainings and research projects. In addition, some psychology students completed internships at locations on and off campus to gain work experience. Because it was nearby, the Veterans Resource Center provided one of the most coveted internships.

## VETERANS RESOURCE CENTER

The Veterans Resource Center (VRC) was an on-campus, one-stop location that fostered and coordinated services and resources for U.S. military veterans, active military members, and their family members. It assisted veterans and service members with obtaining transcripts, completing financial aid applications, and applying for scholarships for enrollment at WIU. It also advocated for student veterans and their opportunities for success through academic and social programs. In addition, it partnered with various university departments, including the Department of Psychology, to increase awareness of specialized mental health services and programs for military service members and their families at the university.

VRC employed six people, including four men and two women, each with their own ties to the military: Matt Schofield, director of VRC and a current Army chaplain; Brittany Wilks, assistant director and an Army veteran; Dylan Busby, coordinator and an Army mechanic; Trevor Jacobs, student coordinator and combat veteran; Nathan Brown, a kinesiology and sports studies intern and combat veteran; and Jane Dailey, a work-study student and daughter of an Army general.

## AMANDA BYRNES, UNDERGRADUATE PSYCHOLOGY STUDENT

Amanda Byrnes was from Peoria, a small city in downstate Illinois. She lived with her mother, father, and younger sister. In the fourth grade, she was the subject of a Division of Family and Children Services (DFCS) case after she came to school with a black eye and bruises around her neck. When a DFCS social worker interviewed Amanda at school, she was too afraid to disclose any information about the abuse by her father. Nevertheless, following the report, Amanda's father was ordered to attend anger management classes. Still the abuse continued. During the years of physical and emotional abuse by her father, Amanda's mother never intervened to protect her and was often verbally abusive as well. However, the abuse by her father abruptly stopped in her sophomore year of high school after a cousin and close friends witnessed him grab Amanda by the neck and slam her to the ground during a family vacation.

Because of what she endured at home, Amanda dealt with significant emotional challenges at school. Although an introverted child, she became combative with peers, even throwing chairs in one incident, and displayed occasional angry outbursts that interrupted class instruction. Despite these challenges, she was bright and able to maintain satisfactory grades.

After graduating from high school in May 2011, Amanda decided to attend WIU, which was about a ninety-minute drive from her home. She was pleased with her decision to begin classes at WIU because most of her high school friends were accepted to the university and would be starting in the fall semester as well. Because of her quiet and shy demeanor, Amanda was relieved to have the support of her friends while making the transition to college.

As a result of her personal experience, Amanda had developed a passion for helping people with mental health challenges resulting from physical or emotional abuse. She decided that pursuing an undergraduate degree in psychology would be a great fit. To her delight, she performed well in her psychology classes and built positive relationships with professors.

## THE PSYCHOLOGY INTERNSHIP

During her senior year at WIU, Amanda was accepted into a competitive psychology internship program. Only twenty students were selected for the program, and they were required to take the prerequisite field course during the fall semester before a field placement in the spring semester. Her biopsychology professor, Josh Stevenson, agreed to serve as her faculty supervisor, and after completing the necessary coursework for the internship program in December of 2014, she began searching for field placement opportunities.

Because Amanda was bright and hardworking, she had little trouble securing an internship. VRC was a coveted internship on campus, and she managed to arrange an interview with the director, Matt Schofield. Impressed by Amanda's ideas for the center, he offered her an internship position on the spot, and she happily accepted. Having a cousin who had trouble finding mental health support services after completing a tour in Iraq, she was especially eager to begin working with military veterans and their families at VRC.

In mid-December 2014, over the holiday break, Amanda began her internship at VRC. Eager to impress, she finished assigned tasks before the deadlines and, with Matt's permission, started working on new projects for the organization. She also developed close friendships with Brittany and Jane, the two women in the office.

By late January, however, Amanda started to notice a pattern in Matt's behavior. He assigned the men major projects, while he assigned Amanda and the other women menial tasks such as typing up his notes or organizing his files. At the same time, she noticed that Matt overstepped professional boundaries. It started with him making sexually inappropriate comments toward Amanda and the other women in the office and quickly escalated to him drawing nude pictures of them and passing these around to the other men in the office. Because of their discomfort with Matt's behavior, Brittany and Jane began working from home, leaving Amanda alone in the office with four men. For her part, she started to collect surreptitious audio recordings and videos of Matt's concerning behavior as evidence. Despite her discomfort, she felt trapped in the placement. *If I don't finish out my internship*, she reflected, *I won't have enough credits to graduate. I mean, this isn't the worst thing that's ever happened to me. He didn't physically hurt me. Is this really that bad?* As much as possible, she tried to ignore Matt's behavior.

## THE APARTMENT INCIDENT

In late April 2015, with only one month to go to complete her internship at VRC, Amanda sat in the office finishing a project.

"Hey, Amanda," Matt interrupted, "I need your help to run an errand."

"Okay," Amanda agreed, aware that no one else was present to help.

As Matt steered his car off campus, he asked about the project Amanda was finishing and commended her efforts. Minutes later Amanda was surprised when Matt pulled into an apartment complex.

"What are we doing here?" Amanda asked, concern in her voice.

"Oh, we're just swinging by my apartment," Matt explained. "I have to grab some things."

"Oh, okay," Amanda hesitated. "I'll just wait in the car."

"No, you can come in. It'll only take a second," Matt promised.

Matt unlocked the apartment door and proceeded down the hallway. But Amanda remained near the front door.

*I don't really like being at Matt's apartment*, Amanda thought as she glanced around the room. *He's my boss.*

"Hey, Amanda!" Matt shouted from the bedroom. "You wanna come help me with this?"

"With what?" Amanda yelled back.

"With one of these boxes," Matt said.

"Oh, you can't get it?" Amanda responded nervously.

"No, can you come help me?" Matt seemed insistent.

Amanda noted that Matt had left the lights off in the bedroom. *He's gonna attack me*—her mind raced—*if I go back there! I don't know what I'm going to walk into.*

"Could you just bring them out here one at a time?" Amanda urged.

"Just come back here!" Matt snapped, with a raised voice.

Instead, Amanda spun and rushed out of the apartment. Once outside, Amanda realized she was sweating and felt her heart racing. She stood near Matt's car and waited for him to come out of the apartment.

*If I go back in there, he's going to attack me and then what?* Amanda struggled with her thoughts. *I have to get out of here.*

A few minutes later Matt returned from the apartment without any boxes.

"You ready?" Matt asked flatly.

*Am I overreacting?* Amanda wondered. *This is bizarre.*

"I need to finish that project," Amanda said out loud.

"Okay," Matt offered, "I'll have to have one of the guys come back and help me."

Later that day and into the evening, Amanda texted with Brittany and Jane about how Matt made her feel unsafe and violated.

## TALKING WITH SUSAN PRIESTLY, DIRECTOR OF STUDENT PROGRAMS

A few days later Amanda received an email from Susan Priestly, Matt's boss and the director of student programs, requesting to meet with her immediately to discuss some VRC issues that had recently come to her attention. Susan had availability that afternoon at 1 P.M. so Amanda agreed to meet. Amanda quickly texted Jane and Brittany to ask if they knew what was going on. They acknowledged having reported Matt's behavior to Susan and suggested she just wanted Amanda's perspective.

"Tell me what's been going on," Susan began. "I heard some things from Brittany and Jane, but I'd really like to hear from you, kinda what your experience has been."

"Telling me he's taking me one place," Amanda said carefully, "but then taking me another. For example, he took me to his apartment one time."

"He took you to his apartment?" Susan sounded surprised.

"Yeah, last Wednesday," Amanda replied.

"What was the purpose of the trip there?" Susan inquired.

"Well, he didn't tell me the reason," Amanda explained.

"So what happened in his apartment?" Susan asked, listening intently.

"I got nervous." Amanda paused. "Then I walked back out to the car."

"Okay, I see," Susan said.

"But there is lots of other stuff going on with Matt as well. There would be times," Amanda explained, "where he would leave the office for non-office-related things and would have us lie to you about where he was going and what he was up to, like running personal errands, doing laundry, going to meet with his girlfriend, and making private calls to meet with a lawyer regarding his ex-wife. He would often take extended smoke breaks."

Susan looked up from taking notes.

"He would take the guys to do things," Amanda emphasized, "and leave the girls back. He would assign us only administrative things, and the guys would get actual projects. He said, 'The women in the office are useless.' That's why he would give the guys the projects."

"I would really like you to type this all up and send it to me. And I really encourage you to meet with the Office of Civil Rights and Diversity," Susan suggested. "Is it okay if I pass your information on to them?"

"Yeah, that's fine," Amanda answered nervously. *Oh my gosh*, she mused, *this is really going to go somewhere. What can of worms did I just open?*

"The things that Brittany and Jane touched on fell more under something that I can handle, but there were some things that you said that concern me. I think you should meet with these people," Susan encouraged.

*Oh crap! Now I'm alone*, Amanda realized. *This isn't just, like, three women coming forward; this is just, like, me.*

"I'll definitely get the email to you," Amanda said cautiously, "but I'll need to think about reporting to that other office."

## TALKING WITH A COUSIN

On the drive home, Amanda called her cousin Margret Hillman to tell her about the conversation with Susan.

"Is it just me or do you kinda get that interpretation that I was kinda set up?" Amanda asked, with a bit of confusion. "Like, Brittany and Jane made me think, like, 'we're all in this together' to get me motivated and empowered to come forward, and once I was ready to come forward they were all, like, 'this is all you.' "

"I kinda do see that," Margret explained. "But also keep in mind these people haven't been there the last few weeks so they don't have the same experiences that you do."

"What do I do?" Amanda asked intensely. "Do I meet with these people, or do I just ignore them? I mean the school year is almost over. I wanna put this internship on my resume, and I want a letter of recommendation from him." Amanda paused. "Or I lose that experience."

"I don't know," Margret said.

"Can I still put that on my resume if there is no point of contact and then I don't get that letter of recommendation that I've been holding out for?"

"I can't answer that for you," Margret responded. "You can make a point either way."

"Ugghhh," Amanda groaned.

## MEETING WITH THE SEMINAR INSTRUCTOR

Later that evening Amanda remembered she had a good relationship with her seminar instructor, Stacy Allen, and emailed her to set up a meeting:

> I've been having trouble with my field instructor, Matt Schofield, and wondered if we could talk.

Stacy responded promptly and agreed to meet with Amanda on campus the following day.

The next morning Amanda knocked on Stacy's office door. After a bit of small talk, Stacy invited Amanda to explain what she was referring to in the email. Amanda recounted several of the key events.

"I believe you," Stacy responded firmly. "That sounds exactly like something that he would say and do based on the interaction I had with him. Have you told your psychology supervisor about this?"

"No," Amanda responded.

"Just to be clear, you haven't mentioned this to him?"

"No, I just really didn't feel comfortable," Amanda explained.

"Okay," Stacy rejoined, "I'm glad you let me know."

"What do I do?" Amanda pleaded.

"Unfortunately, I can't tell you what to do," Stacy explained. "This is entirely up to you, but I can help you think through the issues and try to decide. What would you tell a friend to do in this situation?"

"Well," Amanda said, before pausing and exhaling deeply, "I would tell my friend that they should report, but it's different when you're actually, like, in the situation."

## A CALL FROM THE OFFICE OF CIVIL RIGHTS AND DIVERSITY

Later that day, after meeting with Stacy, Amanda's cell phone rang.

"Hello, Amanda, this is Heidi Donaldson. I'm the assistant director at the Office of Civil Rights and Diversity. Susan forwarded your information to me," Heidi began. "Are you able to come in and meet with me?"

"Well," Amanda said hesitantly, "I suppose I can come in and share my story."

They agreed to meet on Monday, the earliest available date.

*Maybe this is just military culture, and I have to learn to live with it*. After ending the call with Heidi, Amanda started to second-guess herself. *Or was I kinda allowing it since I didn't say it was wrong and didn't speak up?*

The following Monday Amanda walked into the Office of Civil Rights and Diversity and was greeted by Heidi and her assistant, Liz Robinson. They escorted her into a private room for the interview.

"Anything you say with us will be kept confidential unless you decide to pursue action," Heidi assured her.

"What does that look like?" Amanda asked.

"We can move forward with this," Heidi explained, "only if you decide to go public, to attach your name."

"So that means that he will know I'm the one who reported it?" Amanda's voice suddenly became quieter.

"Yes," Heidi said.

*Oh, gosh, I really can't do it now.* Amanda paused, her mind racing. *If it was anonymous, I wouldn't feel so bad. But having my name attached to it, everyone in the office is gonna know, even the guys. And he knows where I live! I can't move forward with this.*

"Can I just share my story with you and then we can kinda go from there," Amanda asked nervously, "if you think it's worth pursuing?"

"Sure," Heidi responded. "That's a good idea."

"Because I really don't wanna start all of this and get my name out there just for something not to happen. And really leave me standing there to take all the backlash."

"We would need your permission first," Heidi assured. "We won't do anything without your permission.

"Okay," Amanda said.

"We've heard stories like this before, and we pursued those. Here are some of the actions that we've taken before," Heidi explained. "Some people received probation, some were let go, and some got the option to quit or be fired. Of course, there have been some cases that didn't get off the ground. Nothing came of them, but most of the time one of those three things happens."

While Amanda recounted her experiences with Matt, Heidi and Liz listened attentively. As she described certain incidents, Amanda played audio recordings and showed video recordings she had collected on her cell phone over the past few months. She also shared emails and screenshots with Heidi and Liz that documented Matt's behaviors in the office.

"Especially with this evidence," Heidi said, "it is more likely that we can take action. The documentation you've collected will be really helpful. But, again, we can't move forward or do anything with this until we have your permission."

"Is there any way," Amanda wondered, "you can move forward with my permission, but I can still remain anonymous?"

"Well," Heidi explained, "he has the right to know who his accuser is."

"That makes sense," Amanda replied, looking down at the floor. "I have to think about it."

"Take your time," Heidi said. "This is a tough decision. But," she added gently, "the school year is coming to a close."

"And I'm graduating," Amanda added.

"Yeah, if you want to take action, I suggest we do it quickly so that this doesn't bleed into your summer. I don't think we'll need to meet again, but I wouldn't want you to be commuting from Peoria to meet with us."

"Right," Amanda nodded.

"We'll be here," Heidi promised, "if there's anything else you want to talk about. If you have any questions, don't hesitate to ask."

"Okay," Amanda offered, "I'll let you know what I decide within a couple days. I don't like to have people waiting on me."

Walking back across campus after the meeting, Amanda weighed the consequences of her decision. *I really want this letter of recommendation*, she thought. *I don't want this whole year to go to waste. Brittany and Jane have completely removed themselves from the office. If I don't do anything, any future women who come to work in that office . . . I'm really just setting them up to be in the same situation that all three of us have been in. I didn't get a warning. This probably could've been stopped before I even made it into the office. But either they didn't feel like they had a case against him, or they didn't feel like they could say something. Protecting the next person—that's worth more to me than a letter of recommendation. It could get worse.*

*But because all the guys are buddy-buddy with him, this might be their word against mine, not just his. Everyone in the office will vouch for him. And I'll just lose any friendships I have with any of those guys. I don't want them to hate me. What if they lie for him? What would I look like? Especially since Jane and Brittany have backed off from this. He knows where I live. What if he just shows up there sometime? If he loses his job, then I would feel really guilty.* Thoughts were swirling around in Amanda's head. *What do I do?*

# 15

## WHOSE BABY?

*L. Bailey King, Melissa C. Reitmeier, and Terry A. Wolfer*

"Well, that's good to know," said the hospital social worker Harper Glendell. Her disappointment was evident in her tone. "Thanks for trying anyway. I appreciate your help."

"I wish I could do more," responded Kinsey Morris, the Hospital Response Team coordinator, as they ended the call.

There was a brief moment of silence in the office as Harper processed what she had just learned and what that meant for their patient.

"So what was that about?" Serena Thompson prompted, anxious to hear where their clients would be placed.

---

This decision case was prepared solely to provide material for class discussion and not to suggest either effective or ineffective handling of the situation depicted. While based on field research regarding an actual situation, names and certain facts may have been disguised to protect confidentiality. The authors wish to thank the case reporter for cooperation in making this account available for the benefit of social work students and practitioners.

*She's not going to take this well.* Harper met Serena's gaze. Taking a steadying breath, she said, "Well, Harmony House isn't taking any new patients because of the COVID-19 pandemic."

"What?" Serena gasped.

## MERCY HOSPITAL SPRINGFIELD EMERGENCY DEPARTMENT

Mercy Hospital Springfield was a not-for-profit, 866-bed hospital located in downtown Springfield, Missouri, that served people throughout southwestern Missouri and northwestern Arkansas. It was part of the Mercy Health System, which spanned four states and was named one of the top five large U.S. health systems for four consecutive years. Specifically, Mercy Hospital Springfield was a Missouri- and Arkansas-designated Level I Trauma Center and Burn Center, as well as having a dedicated Children's Hospital, Cancer Center, Level III Neonatal ICU, and Heart Institute. Staff in Mercy Hospital Springfield's Emergency Department saw over eighty-six thousand patients in 2019.

In the emergency room (ER), social workers played a major role in crisis intervention, discharge planning, and resource coordination for patients in order to prevent unnecessary admissions or readmissions and ensure patients' safety when discharged from the hospital. For example, when a physician or nurse was concerned that a patient might have been a victim of domestic violence, they contacted the ER social worker for a consult. The social worker would then meet with the patient and evaluate whether further services or resources were needed. If children were present during the incident involving domestic violence, the social worker was required to report the incident to the Children's Division of the Missouri Department of Social Services (DSS).

## HARPER GLENDELL, LMSW, EMERGENCY DEPARTMENT SOCIAL WORKER

Harper Glendell was a thirty-one-year-old, white woman from Nixa, a small suburb of Springfield. She received her BA in psychology in 2011 and her MSW in 2014, both from Missouri State University. After graduating from the MSW program and obtaining her social work license, she worked in an inpatient psychiatric facility for one year and then in a community outreach program offered by Mercy Hospital Springfield. She enjoyed working with the community, but after two years, she transferred to the Mercy Hospital Springfield Emergency Department, where she focused on teaching patients how to use available resources or alternate services to prevent unnecessary visits to the ER. She found her time working in community outreach was especially valuable because she could use her community contacts to better support her patients.

While working in the ER, Harper discovered her passion for crisis intervention. She felt at home in the Emergency Department's fast-paced environment, especially when things were stressful and needed rapid responses. She could solve problems quickly when her adrenaline was pumping.

Harper had worked in the ER for two and a half years and was in her second year as a field instructor for MSW students at Missouri State University. She had felt nervous when accepting her first student intern but soon found she enjoyed the teaching process and could develop positive, trusting relationships with interns. In several situations, she thought she learned as much from her student intern as she taught. Recently, she also signed up for classes to begin working toward her LISW.

## SERENA THOMPSON, SOCIAL WORK INTERN

Serena Thompson was a thirty-year-old, African American woman from Ozark, Missouri, about twenty-two miles south of Springfield. Before enrolling in the MSW program at Missouri State University, she worked for two years as a case worker with the Missouri Department of Social Services in the Foster Care Services Unit. During the MSW program, she worked as a parent liaison with the school district in her hometown. She was also a single mother of two boys under the age of ten.

Serena was a highly motivated and engaged student, both in the classroom and at the field placement. Never afraid to ask a question, she had a strong work ethic and was a self-starter. She worked well with the ER staff and treated every patient with respect and care, with special consideration for the children who came through the ER.

Sometimes she would get emotionally invested in a particular case, especially if it involved a mother or a child, but she was able to process these situations in supervision with Harper. In March 2020, Serena was in the final semester of her advanced-practice field placement.

## HARMONY HOUSE

Harmony House was a not-for-profit community organization that provided safe emergency housing, education, and advocacy for families escaping domestic violence. Its services included a twenty-four-hour hotline and crisis intervention, a short-term emergency shelter, long-term transitional housing, case management, outreach, advocacy, and community education. It was the largest domestic violence shelter in Missouri and had provided shelter and support for domestic violence survivors since 1976. Around 50 percent of its income came from grants and contracts. It also received income from contributions (25 percent), fund-raising (14 percent), and foundations (5 percent). In 2019, it answered 2,619 crisis calls and sheltered 858 adults and children.

In 2018, Harmony House created a program called the Hospital Response Team (HRT) that received referrals directly from Mercy Hospital Springfield. When the HRT coordinator received notification from a medical social worker that a patient needed domestic violence services, she or another case worker from Harmony House would meet with the patient in the hospital to complete an initial assessment and help arrange transportation, counseling, and other supportive services. This allowed patients to be directly connected with community services and resources that fit their needs.

## KINSEY MORRIS, HARMONY HOUSE HRT COORDINATOR

Kinsey Morris, a white woman in her early thirties, had obtained her LPC in 2012. She had worked at Harmony House for five years and had served as the HRT coordinator since the program's inception. She was passionate about her work at Harmony House. In addition to completing referrals and assessments, she provided individual and group counseling to domestic violence survivors through Harmony House.

She enjoyed supporting her clients and helping them turn their lives around. During the first two years of the program, Harper and Kinsey developed a positive working relationship. If Harper notified Kinsey of a patient in need, Kinsey would typically arrive at the ER within thirty minutes.

## COVID-19 EFFECTS AND AGENCY RESPONSES

Due to the coronavirus pandemic, many organizations required mitigation strategies for day-to-day operations. For example, if a hospital patient tested positive for COVID-19, Mercy required a family member to pick them up or transported them directly home via a stretcher transport. In the early stages of the pandemic, hospital policies changed several times in response to new information pertaining to COVID-19, causing confusion and an increased burden on staff. At minimum, staff tried to figure out how to care for patients who tested positive for COVID-19 without increasing the risk to themselves or their families. Testing was not readily available during the month of March.

Many community organizations chose to reduce or temporarily eliminate in-person services, reduce staff sizes, or temporarily close due to the uncertainty of the situation. Social workers and their clients found it especially difficult to navigate the situation, as these decisions fluctuated. At the time, Mercy Hospital Springfield did not permit the HRT staff from Harmony to complete in-person assessments at the hospital, so they had to obtain the necessary information over the phone.

## SERENA TAKES THE LEAD

Moments after sitting down at her desk, Harper clicked a notification that blinked on her computer screen. An ER nurse had just sent another domestic violence consult, the second of the day.

"Well, Serena," Harper said as she stretched in her chair, "it looks like we have another DV consult. The patient's name is Alexis Walker, a twenty-one-year-old, African American female. It says here that she sustained an ankle injury during a domestic violence incident with her boyfriend and came to the hospital in an ambulance with some police officers and her baby. Since you just shadowed me on that other DV case this morning, I'm going to let you take the lead on this one."

"Sounds good to me," Serena said, smiling.

Harper gathered her clipboard, intake forms, and favorite pen. "Don't worry," she reassured Serena, "I'll still be with you in case you leave something out or start to feel uncomfortable. I'm here to take over if you need me to."

"Thanks," Serena said, holding her own clipboard with the intake forms as she followed Harper out the office door.

## INTRODUCTIONS AND PATIENT HISTORY

Harper let Serena walk into Alexis's room first. As soon as they entered, Harper noticed two things: there was a toddler waddling around the room, and there was definitely something wrong with Alexis's ankle. It was swollen with dark, splotchy bruises already spreading up into her calf.

"Devon," Alexis begged the toddler, "just sit still for one second!" She winced when she moved the leg with the injured ankle.

"Hi, Ms. Walker, my name is Serena. I'm a master's-level social work student intern. Would you mind speaking with me, or would you prefer speaking to my supervisor?"

Harper was impressed with Serena's professional demeanor. *I never even instructed you to ask Alexis who she wanted to speak with. Good on you!*

"No, that's fine," Alexis replied. "I'll speak with you. Call me Alexis."

"Okay, great," Serena said. "So we're here to talk with you because the doctor was concerned that there was some sort of domestic violence incident."

"Yes, my boyfriend ran over my foot with my car," Alexis replied, her voice wavering a little. Harper noticed her eyes were swollen from crying and her clothes were disheveled with dirt stains here and there.

"I'm so sorry that happened to you." Serena's expression was one of genuine concern. "It says the police came with you and the ambulance to the ER. Did you make a police report?"

Alexis sniffled and wiped her nose with the back of her hand as she nodded. "Yeah, I did."

"Do you mind if we get that case number from you?" Serena asked.

*You're doing really well so far*, Harper thought to herself, *and even remembered to ask for the case number!*

Alexis nodded again and dug a crumpled business card out of her pocket.

Serena wrote down the case number handwritten on the back. "Thanks." Serena handed the card back to Alexis. "Do you mind going into some detail about what happened between you and your boyfriend?"

"Well, my boyfriend, Lawrence, was driving me to work and was going to drop Devon off with his mom—Lawrence's mom—on his way to work. I work at a call center downtown, and Lawrence works at UPS. But on the way, I don't know what happened; it's like he flipped a switch all the sudden." There was a tremor in Alexis's voice, and she began to cry. She tried to wrangle the toddler to sit in her lap, but he started squirming to be let down.

Serena got the boy's attention, and he waddled over to her. She flipped over one of her forms to the blank side and handed the boy her pen. He squealed, grabbed the pen, and plopped down on the floor to scribble on the paper.

"Thanks," Alexis said quietly, wiping her tears away with her sleeve.

Harper passed Alexis a box of tissues that was already in the room. *You look so young*, Harper mused. *I couldn't imagine going through all that and having to take care of a baby.*

"It's okay. You're safe here," Serena said with a comforting tone. "What do you mean he flipped a switch?"

Alexis took a couple tissues and blew her nose before she continued. "He just said he changed his mind. He didn't want me working anymore, and he didn't want me going nowhere."

"What happened next?" Serena prompted.

"He kept driving. I tried to get him to pull over, but he refused. He started yelling crazy stuff, so I called 911."

"What was he saying?" Serena asked.

"He was yelling stuff like 'We're gonna go on this high-speed chase and if we crash and the baby gets hurt, I don't care' and 'We're both going out.' I know the 911 lady heard it. We finally heard some sirens, and I guess that freaked him out, so he pulled into a McDonald's parking lot. I jumped out the car right then and went to get Devon out the backseat, but Lawrence grabbed Devon's arm and yanked him back. Then he took off. That's when he ran over my ankle." Alexis pointed at her injured ankle.

Harper noticed Serena struggling to hide her shocked expression. It appeared Serena was trying to take everything in but remain professional. *This is a lot to process*, Harper thought. *I should have let you take the first DV case from this morning! This one is getting complicated with so many details. I hope you don't feel overwhelmed . . . No, no*, Harper caught herself, *I just need to trust your ability and be here to support you.*

"So how did you get Devon back?" Serena asked, glancing at the gurgling toddler wielding her pen.

"When Lawrence took off, I screamed after him to give me my baby back. I couldn't put weight on my foot and kept falling, but I made sure to scream as loud as I could 'cause I saw a bunch of people in the parking lot. They saw the whole thing. I think that's what made him turn around—all those people watching. He basically shoved Devon out the window at me and then drove off!" Alexis's voice steadily grew louder. "He took everything—my car, my phone, my wallet, my house keys! Everything!"

Confused, Devon looked up at the sound of his mother's voice and started to whimper. Serena noticed the boy's distress and moved to comfort him.

"Alexis," Harper interjected, trying to keep her voice even and calm. *This is getting out of hand*, Harper thought, *and Serena is completely distracted with the little boy.* "The important thing right now is that you and Devon are here and you're safe. I think I saw that the doctor wants to get a couple scans of that ankle to figure out what needs to be done. Do you have anyone you can call that could take care of Devon if you need surgery?"

Alexis's shoulders drooped, and she wrung the tissues she gripped tightly in her hands. "I guess I can call my mom. She lives about an hour away, near Carthage, but she doesn't have a car. If it turns out Devon has to stay with her, then we'll just figure it out. I don't have my phone though. It was in my car."

"Serena and I can find a phone for you to use," Harper reassured Alexis, glancing at Serena to see how she was doing. Serena had Devon sitting on her lap, drawing on the back of her forms as she held the clipboard. "I know you said your mom lives near Carthage, but do you think you could stay with her until the police are able to find your boyfriend? I don't think it's safe for you to go back home today."

Alexis shook her head. "I can't leave. I really need to keep my job. I'm probably already in trouble for not showing up today. Lawrence took my car, so I don't have a way to get to my mom's, even if I wanted to." Alexis started to cry again.

"Hey, it's okay. We work with people in all kinds of situations," Harper said gently. "We'll figure out a place you can go where you'll be safe. That's our job."

## COORDINATING SERVICES

When Harper and Serena left the room, Harper could tell Serena was struggling to maintain her composure.

"What are we going to do with the baby?" Serena asked immediately as they started walking toward the office.

"What do you mean? Alexis's mom will come get the baby if Alexis needs surgery," Harper replied.

"Yeah, but what about in the meantime?" Serena pressed. "I mean, she still has to get those scans. And I didn't see any kind of diaper bag in the room or any toys for him to play with."

"Oh, you're right." Harper paused momentarily, surprised by Serena's observations and a little concerned by the sharp tone of her voice. "Good point." *I didn't think about that*, Harper mused. *I guess you're more aware of stuff like that because you're a mom, too, but don't let your emotions take over. Maybe you see too much of yourself in this case.*

"I'm sure the Emergency Department's pediatric unit could lend us some stuff," Serena continued in a rush, cutting through Harper's thoughts as she brainstormed out loud. "They have to have some sort of donation program for children's toys and other supplies. I'll run over there now and talk to their social worker. We'll figure something out." Serena suddenly turned to leave, catching Harper off guard.

"Whoa, hang on a sec!" Harper had to stop her.

Serena turned around expectantly.

"That's a great idea, and I'm glad you're excited to help," Harper explained, "but we also need to talk through our next steps before jumping too far ahead."

Serena nodded, but Harper could tell something was off. It just seemed like Serena wasn't really engaged or interested in the conversation. *Should I say something about your obvious emotional investment with this case now or wait until later? Your own experience with having kids can be helpful, but is it interfering with your ability to prioritize the patient's needs?* Harper quickly decided to deal with the patient first and made a mental note to process the case with Serena later.

"Alexis said she doesn't have anywhere to stay," Harper continued. "So while you go to the pediatric unit, I'll call Kinsey with the HRT and let her know we've got a DV case for her. When you get back, we'll set them up with stuff for the baby, and we'll have to find a phone for Alexis to use. Is there anything else?"

"Nope, not that I can think of," Serena said with a shrug. She casually stepped backward as if to suggest she was ready for this conversation to be over.

"Meet me back in the office when you're done," Harper said, trying to keep her tone neutral.

Serena immediately turned around. "I'll see you in a bit!" she called over her shoulder. Harper watched her walk briskly down the hallway toward the pediatric unit.

As Harper made her way back to her office, she wondered, *How can I bring up Serena's emotional investment in this case in supervision without offending or upsetting her? I'm glad she feels comfortable and confident enough to think of solutions on her own, but she's still a student. She can't just run off to do stuff on her own. How much independence should I give her? Was it a mistake letting her take the lead on this case?*

## REACHING OUT

Harper didn't have to look up Kinsey's number when she sat down at her computer; she had it memorized. She started dialing as soon as she got back to her desk. *I know Harmony House has changed some of its operations in response to COVID, but it's my primary resource for DV cases. Kinsey should at least be able to help coordinate a place for Alexis to stay.* Kinsey answered on the fourth ring.

"This is Kinsey with Harmony House. How may I help you?"

"Hey, Kinsey, it's Harper over at the ER. I've got a case I need your help on. I know you can't come up here, but there's got to be something we can do. This patient just had a pretty traumatic altercation with her boyfriend and is in the ER with her eighteen-month-old son. She's got nothing and nowhere to go." Harper bit her lip, hoping Kinsey could work her usual magic.

"That's horrible, Harper," Kinsey said. "Yeah, I can't come up there, but can I do an assessment with her over the phone? So I can at least get her in the system? Things are getting tight with the whole pandemic situation going on, so I can't guarantee anything, but we can at least try."

Harper wasn't thrilled with Kinsey's reply. Her tone wasn't encouraging, but Harmony House operated the largest shelter in Springfield. If any place was going to have some resources, it would be Harmony House. "Alexis doesn't have a phone right now, but we'll find one for her to use and we'll give you a call," Harper replied.

"Sounds great. I'll be on the lookout for your call," Kinsey said.

## THE CALL BACK

Harper and Serena found a phone for Alexis so she could call Kinsey for the assessment and her mother in case she needed surgery. Thankfully, her scans indicated that she didn't need surgery. All they needed now was a safe place for her to go once she was discharged from the hospital.

"Kinsey said it shouldn't take long for her to talk to the shelter," Serena said impatiently. "That was two hours ago."

"She might be talking to several people. It may take a while," Harper reminded her. "By the way, I want to let you know that you did a really good job of thinking on your feet earlier by getting those supplies for the baby from the pediatric unit. You know we try to treat the whole patient here, and you recognized that taking care of the baby was an important part of taking care of Alexis."

"I just thought of my own kids," Serena said with a shrug, "and how I would want them to be taken care of if I were in Alexis's shoes. I don't know what I would do if my children's dad did something like that." Serena shook her head as she started flipping through some paperwork. "I hope he gets the punishment he deserves. If it were one of my babies, he'd better pray that the cops find him before I do."

Harper didn't know what to say, so she went back to writing up her notes.

About five minutes later Harper's phone rang loudly, making both of them jump. She noticed it was Kinsey's number.

"Hey, Kinsey," Harper answered. "I hope you have some good news for us." She glanced at Serena sitting on the other side of her desk. Serena looked up from some paperwork expectantly.

"Hey, Harper, um, actually I've got some not so good news." Kinsey sounded serious.

*Uh oh.* "Uh, okay. What's the bad news?" Harper asked. Serena set her pen and paperwork to the side, concern spreading across her face.

"Well," Kinsey explained, "I called the shelter, and they are no longer accepting new patients for their facilities due to COVID."

*If Harmony House isn't taking new patients, what about the other shelters?* Harper felt the floor drop from beneath her. She stared at the phone receiver in disbelief. *Where's our patient going to go?*

"Hold on a sec," Harper said as she tried to wrap her mind around this unexpected development. "When did they decide this? I haven't heard anything about it."

"Today," Kinsey replied. "Harmony House sent out the directive today . . . like this morning. They're not the first though. A lot of the boarding homes and community care homes aren't taking new people because of COVID."

"Well, that's good to know," Harper said, disappointment evident in her tone. "Thanks for trying anyway. I appreciate your help."

"I wish I could do more," Kinsey responded and ended the call.

There was a brief moment of silence in the office as Harper processed what she had just learned and what that meant for their patient.

"So what was that about?" Serena prompted anxiously.

*You're not going to take this well.* Harper met Serena's gaze. Taking a steadying breath, she said, "Well, Harmony House isn't taking any new patients because of the pandemic."

"What?" Serena's gasped.

"They just can't take the risk of bringing new people in when there's no way to know if that person is infected or has come in contact with other people who are infected," Harper explained, rubbing her temples. Then she added, more to herself than to Serena, "I wish the hospital would hurry up and get those COVID tests. If we were able to test her, we could prove she doesn't have COVID and the shelter would be able to take her."

"Now what are we supposed to do?" Serena asked, her voice rising in frustration as she gestured broadly. "What if we can't find a place for the mom? She can't go back home—the police haven't caught her boyfriend. He could be there waiting for her! What are we going to do with the baby? That baby doesn't deserve to be taken by DSS, and I should know. I worked for DSS, and I know how they operate. We need to find a safe place for this mom to stay because that baby does *not* need to go into the system."

Harper let Serena vent for a few moments. She appreciated that Serena felt comfortable enough to express her emotions and thoughts. Overall, Harper thought it was good for Serena to get some of those emotions out before seeking a solution, but she was worried about the intensity of Serena's response.

"Serena," Harper said, trying to maintain a calm demeanor, "everything will be okay. We will figure out what to do."

*So much for an easy case. If I'm honest with myself, I'm feeling angry, too. These organizations are supposed to be a safety net to support people at their most vulnerable. I get why they're taking the precaution—no one really knows what's going on with COVID—but if we had tests like we're supposed to, we could have tested our patient and proved to the shelter that its perfectly safe to let her stay. On top of everything else, Serena is taking this case way too personally. How am I supposed to balance this crisis situation and take care of my student? What am I going to do?*

# CONTRIBUTORS

Sara J. English, BA (Columbia College [SC]), MSW (Winthrop University), PhD (University of South Carolina) is an assistant professor at the Winthrop University College of Arts and Sciences, Department of Social Work. She teaches courses on foundational principles of social work and advanced social work practice. Her research interests include environmental and disaster preparedness and response, especially for older or isolated persons; social supports; and ethical practice.

Brian D. Graves, BA and BS (University of Georgia), MSW (University of South Carolina), is a PhD student and research assistant at the University of Georgia School of Social Work. His research interests include criminal justice policy, reentry and reintegration for marginalized populations, and social work in criminal justice settings. His field experiences include the nonprofit sector as well as substance abuse education and prevention.

Linda Ayscue Gupta, BA (University of North Carolina at Chapel Hill), MSW and PhD in media, art, and text (Virginia Commonwealth University), LCSW, currently serves as an adjunct faculty member at the VCU School of Social Work, teaching courses on social work practice and clinical practice. She recently retired as associate professor of teaching and coordinator of the distance education option in the MSW Program. Her teaching and research interests include trauma assessment and intervention, narrative therapy, narrative hypertext, virtual reality and immersive learning, and distance learning and online curriculum development. She served as a field instructor for several years while working as a mental health services provider.

Maria L. Hogan, BSW (Roberts Wesleyan College), MSW (University of South Carolina), LCSW, is a therapist who has focused her clinical work in residential settings, including a drug and alcohol rehabilitation center and an eating disorder treatment center. She has also worked in an overseas setting with stigmatized women. Her research interests include cultural competency, trauma-informed care, and religion and spirituality in social work practice.

Abbie D. Kinnebrew, BA (Wesleyan University), MSW (Virginia Commonwealth University), is an associate professor in teaching at the Virginia Commonwealth University School of Social Work. She taught in field education and served as a full-time field liaison for nine years. She has also taught classroom and online courses in social work practice, emotional and behavioral disorders, and evidence-based practice with children and adolescents. Her practice experience focused on work with children, adolescents, and their families who have experienced complex and chronic trauma.

Robert Jay Palmer, BA (California State University, Fullerton), MSW (California State University, Long Beach), PhD (University of South Carolina), is a professor at the Winona State University Social Work Department. He teaches courses on social work practice at the BSW level. He has served as a director of field education, a field liaison for numerous social work placements, and an off-site field instructor for BSW and MSW students.

Meredith C. F. Powers, BSW (University of North Carolina at Wilmington), MSW (University of North Carolina at Chapel Hill), PhD (University of South Carolina), is an assistant professor at the University of North Carolina at Greensboro Department of Social Work. She teaches courses on diversity and vulnerable populations, environmental justice, and international social work.

Her research interests include climate justice, environmental racism, diversity, equity and inclusion, environmental migration, social work with immigrants and refugees, and the professional socialization of social workers. She has served as a field instructor, field liaison, and BSW field education seminar instructor.

Melissa C. Reitmeier, BA, MSW, and PhD (University of South Carolina), is an associate clinical professor and director of field education at the University of South Carolina College of Social Work. She teaches courses on field education, interprofessional behavioral health, motivational interviewing, and social work practice. Her research interests include the intersection of social work and field education and training programs targeting behavioral health needs (mental health and substance abuse). She has served as an on-site and off-site field instructor and field liaison for numerous students. Currently, she also is chair of the Council on Social Work Education's Council on Field Education.

Tamara Estes Savage, BS (University of North Carolina at Chapel Hill), BSW (University of North Carolina at Wilmington), MSW and PhD (University of South Carolina), is an assistant professor at the University of North Carolina at Pembroke Department of Social Work. She teaches courses on quantitative and qualitative research methods, human behavior in the social environment, and rural social work and a social work field education seminar. Her primary research interests are social exclusion, social and cultural capital, effects of racism on health (especially for African American dialysis patients), and homelessness among higher education students. She has served as a field liaison and field instructor for numerous students.

Janessa Steele, BA (Covenant College), MSW (University of South Carolina), LMSW, is a human services coordinator for the South Carolina Department of Mental Health. She serves patients with a wide range of treatment needs through multiple modalities, including eye movement desensitization and reprocessing therapy. She also serves as a field instructor for social work field placements.

Betty L. Wilson, BA (Claflin University), MSW (University of South Carolina), LMSW, is a PhD student at the University of South Carolina College of Social Work. Her research interests include community-police relations, historical and racial trauma, mental health disparities, and community and family resilience. She has served as a field liaison and an off-site field instructor for several social work placements.

Terry A. Wolfer, BA (Concordia University [NE]), MSW (Ohio State University), PhD (University of Chicago), ACSW, is a professor and interim associate dean for curriculum at the University of South Carolina College of Social Work. He teaches courses on social work practice, program and practice evaluation, and qualitative research methods. His research interests include social work education, the case method of teaching, and religion and spirituality in social work practice. He has served as a field liaison for numerous social work placements and as an off-site field instructor for congregation-based social work placements.

# INDEX

CPSIA information can be obtained
at www.ICGtesting.com
Printed in the USA
JSHW011442051222
34356JS00001B/108

9 780231 201452